Ozu's *Tokyo Story*

CAMBRIDGE FILM HANDBOOKS SERIES

General Editor

Andrew Horton, *Loyola University, New Orleans*

Each CAMBRIDGE FILM HANDBOOK contains essays by leading film scholars and critics that focus on a single film from a variety of theoretical, critical, and contextual perspectives. This "prism" approach is designed to give students and general readers valuable background and insight into the cinematic, artistic, cultural, and sociopolitical importance of selected films. It is also intended to help readers grasp the nature of critical and theoretical discourse on cinema as an art form, a visual medium, and a cultural product. Filmographies and select bibliographies are included to aid readers in their own exploration of the film under consideration.

Ozu's
Tokyo Story

Edited by

David Desser

CAMBRIDGE
UNIVERSITY PRESS

PUBLISHED BY THE PRESS SYNDICATE OF THE UNIVERSITY OF CAMBRIDGE
The Pitt Building, Trumpington Street, Cambridge CB2 1RP, United Kingdom

CAMBRIDGE UNIVERSITY PRESS
The Edinburgh Building, Cambridge CB2 2RU, United Kingdom
40 West 20th Street, New York, NY 10011-4211, USA
10 Stamford Road, Oakleigh, Melbourne 3166, Australia

First published 1997

Printed in the United States of America

Typeset in Stone Serif

Library of Congress Cataloging-in-Publication Data
Ozu's *Tokyo Story*, / edited by David Desser.
p.   cm. – (Cambridge film handbooks series)
Filmography: p.
Includes bibliographical references.
ISBN 0-521-48204-6. – ISBN 0-521-48435-9 (pbk.)
1. *Tokyo monogatari* (Motion picture)   2. Ozu, Yasujiro, 1903–1963 –
Criticism and interpretation.   I. Desser, David.   II. Series.
PN1997.T5953092   1997
791.43'72 – dc20   96-46113
                                                                    CIP

*A catalog record for this book is available from
the British Library.*

ISBN 0-521-48204-6 hardback
ISBN 0-521-48435-9 paperback

Contents

Contributors

Darrell William Davis received his Ph.D. in cinema from the University of Wisconsin, Madison. A revised version of his dissertation, "Picturing Japaneseness: Monumental Style and National Identity in Prewar Japanese Cinema," has been published by Columbia University Press. Davis held a fellowship at the Getty Center for the History of Art and Humanities in Los Angeles. Before that, he was film and video curator at the Honolulu Academy of Arts. He has published articles on Japanese cinema in the *East–West Film Journal* and *Wide Angle* and is a contributor to *Cinematic Landscapes*. He was born and raised in Tokyo.

David Desser received a Ph.D. in cinema studies from the University of Southern California in 1981. Since that time he has taught film at the University of Illinois, Urbana-Champaign, where he is currently Professor of Cinema Studies and Speech Communication. The author or editor of six books and more than fifty articles in anthologies, scholarly journals, reference guides, and encyclopedias, Desser is best known for his work on Japanese cinema. This work includes *The Samurai Films of Akira Kurosawa, Eros plus Massacre: An Introduction to the Japanese New*

Wave Cinema, and the coedited anthologies *Reframing Japanese Cinema: Authorship, Genre, History* and *Cinematic Landscapes: Observations on the Visual Arts and Cinema in China and Japan.* He is currently the editor of *Cinema Journal* and continues to work on a number of projects related to Japanese film.

Linda C. Ehrlich holds a Ph.D. in Japanese studies and theater from the University of Hawaii, where she wrote her dissertation on the films of Mizoguchi. She teaches film, theater, and Japanese language at Case Western Reserve University. She has published extensively on Japanese cinema in such journals as *Japan Forum, Post Script,* the *East–West Film Journal, Film Quarterly,* and *Cinemaya.* She is the coeditor of *Cinematic Landscapes.* She has spent more than two years in Japan over the course of her graduate studies and professional work.

Kathe Geist received a Ph.D. in art history from the University of Michigan and has taught film studies and/or art history at Illinois State University and in Japan, where she taught for two years in Nagoya. She currently teaches art history at the Berklee College of Music in Boston. She is the author of *The Cinema of Wim Wenders: From Paris, France to Paris, Texas* and has published articles on Ozu in *Film Quarterly* and the *East–West Film Journal,* as well as in *Reframing Japanese Cinema* (edited by Arthur Nolletti, Jr., and David Desser) and *Cinematic Landscapes* (edited by Linda C. Ehrlich and David Desser).

Hasumi Shigehiko is perhaps the most widely known and highly regarded Japanese scholar of cinema and popular culture in Japan. He teaches literature, film, and cultural studies at Tokyo University, Japan's most prestigious and influential institution of higher learning. His volume on Ozu (*Kantoku Ozu Yasujiro*) is the most respected work on the filmmaker written in Japanese. He engages influential Western work on Ozu (that of Paul Schrader and Donald Richie) to discuss the ways in which certain cultural and critical assumptions underlying Western perceptions of Ozu are open to question.

Arthur Nolletti, Jr., is Professor of English and Film at Framingham State College in Massachusetts. He is the author of many publications about film and is on the editorial board of *Film Criticism,* in which he has regularly published articles on Japanese cinema and for which he edited a special issue on that topic. He is the coeditor of *Reframing Japanese Cinema* and codirector of the History of Japanese Cinema in English project for the University of Hawaii Press.

Kathleen Shigeta is currently Director of Household Affairs for her family of one husband and three children at their home in Okayama, Japan. Her translations include *Autumn in the Tyrols,* published in *Five Plays by Kishida Kunio* (1995 edition).

Ozu's *Tokyo Story*

DAVID DESSER

Introduction

A FILMMAKER FOR ALL SEASONS

An aging couple, Hirayama Shukichi and his wife, Tomi,[1] living in retirement in the port city of Onomichi, prepare for a train trip to Tokyo to visit their children. A stopover to see a son in Osaka is to be followed by a stay with their eldest son, Koichi, a doctor. Their quiet preparations and gentle banter set a tone of contemplation and nostalgia. Once in Tokyo, however, they realize that Koichi, living in a poor suburb and with a small pediatric practice, is hardly the success they thought he was and seems barely to have time for them. Their daughter Shige, owner of a beauty salon, seems even less interested in their company; indeed, she appears to be outright resentful of their presence.

Koichi and Shige send their parents to Atami, a hot springs resort highly unsuitable for this elderly couple. When they return early to Tokyo, neither Koichi nor Shige is willing to take them in. Only their daughter-in-law, Noriko, a war widow, seems genuinely loving and kind to them; she invites Tomi to stay at her small apartment, while Shukichi must stay at an old friend's. When a drunken Shukichi and his friend are brought to Shige's home by the police, the anger and disappointment the parents feel toward their children and the children toward their parents send the old Hirayamas back home.

1

On the way home, Tomi is taken ill. A stopover in Osaka to recover for the moment finds the old couple reflecting on their life with a mixture of bitterness and resignation. When the Hirayamas return home, Tomi gets worse. Their youngest daughter, Kyoko, still living at home, sends for her brothers, sister, and sister-in-law. Shortly after their arrival in Onomichi, Tomi dies. Only Kyoko and Noriko seem genuinely saddened. As Noriko prepares to return to Tokyo, the widowed Shukichi extends his gratitude to her for her love and kindness and urges her to remarry. Noriko's contemplative journey home ends the film.

That is the simple plot of Ozu Yasujiro's *Tokyo Story* (*Tokyo monogatari*, 1953). Little of this description would indicate that the film is generally acknowledged to be one of the greatest ever made, as indicated, for example, by *Sight and Sound* magazine's respected surveys of film critics. It is probably the best-known film directed by Ozu Yasujiro, both in the West and in Japan. Ozu himself, at least since the middle of the 1970s, has been considered one of Japan's best known and most respected directors in the West; in Japan his status as a major filmmaker was established by 1932, and he remained preeminent among film directors until his death in 1963. His position in the pantheon of Japanese film directors in Japan and the West is unmatched.

Ozu's recognition in the West was a long time in coming compared with that of many Japanese directors working in the 1950s and 1960s. The success of *Rashomon* at the 1951 Venice Film Festival should not make us oblivious to the reality that Japanese producers and distributors created films almost specifically for export to the burgeoning film festival and "art theater" circuit in the United States and around the world, or else sought in their massive output of the 1950s and early 1960s suitable films for export.[2] Such films for export were far more often than not period films, costume dramas, portrayals of the world of the samurai or the geisha. Though Ozu's first film, *The Sword of Penitence* (*Zange no yaiba*, 1927), was a period piece, he never made another one. So as films like *Ugetsu* (Mizoguchi Kenji,

1953), *Gate of Hell* (*Jigokumon*, Kinugasa Teinosuke, 1953), and
the Samurai trilogy (1954–5) by Inagaki Hiroshi were winning
accolades in the West for their lush visual style or exotic appeal,
Ozu quietly went about the business of directing films, typically
one and sometimes two per year starting in 1948.[3] For the Japanese exporters of films to the West, Ozu, it appeared, was just
"too Japanese." That this was far from the truth, that the West
responded to Ozu with as much enthusiasm as ever a Japanese
audience did, became clear only after his death.

As the Japanese film industry declined in the 1960s, the export market paradoxically increased, at least in the United States
because of a precipitous decline in Hollywood's output and the
American film industry's growing inability to reach a target audience. A more demanding college and college-educated audience
began turning its back on the perceived immaturity and escap-
ism of Hollywood and found in foreign films, from France, Italy,
and Sweden, among other countries, an intellectual content and
maturity of themes absent from Hollywood's wheezing attempts
to hold on to its former glory. Thus an audience for Japanese
films was ready and waiting. The showing of a handful of Ozu's
films in the mid-1960s at festivals, museums, and New York
theaters gradually revealed a director seemingly at odds with the
wandering swordsmen and magnificently costumed women that
defined the Japanese cinema for some. Here was a director so
steeped in contemporary Japanese culture as to be making films
without concessions to an international mass audience. That
Ozu was, in fact, very much in tune with the Japanese mass
audience (though his films were not box-office giants in the year
of their release) made U.S. intellectuals excited about coming to
terms with a foreign culture that could produce a filmmaker of
this originality and particularity. That his films were relatively
plotless and steeped in everyday life made them seem if not part
of, then related to, the French New Wave or the severe style
and themes of Michelangelo Antonioni and Ingmar Bergman.
Seemingly endless arguments over Ozu's "Japaneseness," his
place in world cinema history, and the depths of his stories and

themes testify to this filmmaker's international significance and universality.

The respect accorded both *Tokyo Story* and Ozu himself stems from a number of factors. The film is, paradoxically, both intensely insular and immensely universal. Rarely has a film been so immersed in specifics of setting and period, so thoroughly pervaded by the culture from which it was produced. Indeed, so completely does the film derive from particularities of Japanese culture – marriage, family, setting – that critics have argued over the film's basic themes. Is it about the breakup of the traditional Japanese family in the light of postwar changes (increased urbanization and industrialization, which have led to the decline of the extended family)? Or is it about the inevitabilities of life: children growing up, getting married, moving away from home, having children of their own, leaving their aging parents behind? Of course, though the film is set in a specific time and place, such questions concerning the breakdown of tradition and the changes that life inevitably brings are universal in their appeal. Like *Bicycle Thieves* (*Ladri di biciclette*) made just a few years earlier, *Tokyo Story* derives its power from both its unique setting and the universality of its characters and theme.

For film scholars and students, the pleasures and power of *Tokyo Story*, indeed of Ozu's oeuvre in its entirety, stem not just from the way in which the film's thematic range is steeped in Japanese culture, but also, and perhaps more interestingly, from its stylistic practices. Under the influence of critics and historians, ranging from film-critic-turned-director Paul Schrader to Donald Richie (the best-known and most prolific scholar-critic of the Japanese cinema), Noel Burch, and David Bordwell, the Western fascination with Ozu has revolved around his cinematic techniques, which, like his films' themes, have been endlessly debated and discussed. One debate has centered on his proclivity for the low camera position, said by some to reproduce the typical Japanese perspective of someone sitting on a tatami mat. A more intense debate has concerned his use of "empty shots," said by many to reproduce the worldview of Zen Buddhism or to reflect the modernist fascination with surface and materiality. In addition to issues of camera placement and mise-en-scène, critics have noted Ozu's narrative strategy whereby plot is completely deemphasized. This is considered by some to deny the cause–effect chain that is a function of Western logocentrism, individualism, and bourgeois capitalism, or to draw viewer attention away from results and toward process. These are just some of the issues that situate Ozu as a filmmaker with a unique and uniquely important cinematic consciousness. Moreover, Ozu is prized by so many film scholars and critics because he offers an alternative to mainstream American cinema (the vaunted "classical Hollywood cinema").

Thus *Tokyo Story* can be appreciated as a film with universal appeal in its story of aging parents and their disappointments with their children and their lives or as a paradigm of the unique cinema of Ozu. From either perspective, the film is rich in its implications.

NARRATIVE AND SPACE IN *TOKYO STORY*

One technique whereby a film viewer or "reader" learns to appreciate the particularities of a film is to make comparisons, implicitly or explicitly, with other films. In other words, the viewer analyzes the film against a set of "norms." In film studies, those norms are based on the classical Hollywood cinema, and indicate not what is right or wrong, but what is usual, typical, or standard, but without value judgment. (For example, there is nothing good or bad about an "inch" or a "meter"; either is just a standard measurement.) Thus the characteristics of "ordinary" American film may be used to grasp the uniqueness of Ozu's cinema in general and of *Tokyo Story* in particular.

What the typical viewer, Western or Japanese, ordinarily first realizes about Ozu's films is the apparent lack of plot – not of story, but of story-events. Plot in American cinema is usually tied to the dramatic, the action-packed, the revelatory; it relies on a rigid chain of cause and effect from which extraneous detail is eliminated in the interest of "moving the plot along." Not so in an Ozu film, where "extraneous event" is an almost meaningless term because the film is made up of a series of moments, cumulative in their power and their emotional effect, but not causal, not story-driven. The clearest indication of how this works can be found, so to speak, precisely in the sorts of things Ozu leaves out.

An important narrative principle for Ozu is the ellipsis, the omission of plot material or even an event. In films like *Late Spring* (*Banshun,* 1949) and *An Autumn Afternoon* (*Samma no aji,* 1962) the plot point, the dramatic highlight, to which the film has been leading, is elided: these films about a daughter who ought to marry never show the husband-to-be when the daughter agrees to marry. In *Tokyo Story* we are aware of various sorts of ellipses. There is the "minor ellipsis," in which certain plot points are dropped. For instance, in one scene, the two oldest children discuss sending their parents on a trip to Atami (Figure 1). This is followed by a shot of people on a seawall (Figure 2), then by a shot of the sea seen from an interior (Figure 3), then a shot down the length of a hallway, and, finally, a shot of the old couple in a hotel (Figure 4). Thus we see that the parents are already at the spa, and we understand that Ozu has eliminated scenes in which the parents are told about the trip, are put on a train to Atami, and arrive at the resort.

This sort of minor ellipsis is common in worldwide cinema, but nevertheless needs highlighting here. It involves the principle of retrospectivity, the active participation of viewers, who must constantly reintegrate themselves into the action, reorient themselves within filmic time and space. The greater the ellipsis the more active, the more involved we must be. In Ozu's films, the variety of ellipses requires that we pay attention. For instance, Ozu often uses what may be called a "surprise ellipsis." Here plot points prepared for by dialogue and action are, in fact, elided. At the start of *Tokyo Story* the parents discuss changing trains in Osaka and thus seeing their younger son, who lives and works there. The next scene begins in Tokyo at the home of the older son, and shortly thereafter the parents arrive. The Osaka visit discussed by the parents is thus never shown, although we learn that the rendezvous did, in fact, take place. Preparing us for a scene that never occurs onscreen is a daring strategy. Even more daring is the fact that the scene has occurred offscreen. Talked about, prepared for, clearly mentioned, it is then simply elided.

More daring yet is the "dramatic ellipsis," whereby something important has occurred, but offscreen. In *Tokyo Story* this is the parents' arrival in Osaka on the return trip and their overnight stay because the mother has become ill. We learn about their arrival secondhand, as it were, after the fact, from the second son, who mentions that they are now in Osaka because of the mother's illness. By the time we see the couple, they are already at the son's home and the mother is, for the moment, recovering (though, somewhat rare for Ozu, this prepares us for her eventual demise). The point is that the drama of her illness, the sudden change in plans, is not shown. As just mentioned, the first Osaka trip, which we expect to see, is not shown (something not atypical of Ozu). The second, unexpected stop in Osaka, is shown, however.

Now if the sorts of things Ozu eliminates are often the sorts of things most American films are specifically built around, moments of intense emotion surrounding events like reunions, marriages, illness, we may need to account for this difference. Ozu's strategies are rooted in elements of the Japanese aesthetic tradition – the deemphasis of drama and the elision of plot elements in theatrical works, the emphasis on mood and tone instead of story in literature. Some of the essays in this volume discuss Ozu's films in relation to other modes of Japanese art, history, and religion. For now, the important point is the manner in which the story, the drama, is told differently than in American cinema, if just a bit differently.

Ozu's spatial composition, specifically his "screen direction" and "mismatched action," can similarly be linked to elements of the Japanese aesthetic tradition. We will look first, briefly, at the way Ozu handles transitional spaces.

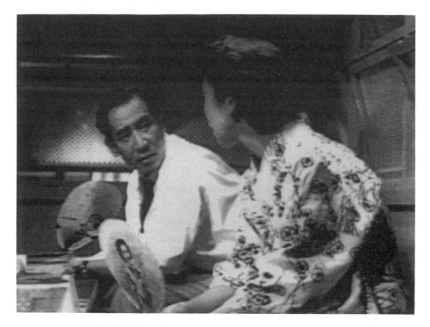

FIGURE I

FIGURE 2

FIGURE 3

FIGURE 4

Transitional spaces are linked to retrospectivity in general and often ellipsis in particular. Instead of a direct cut between scenes, Ozu often finds "intermediate spaces." These are sometimes intermediate in a literal sense, in that they fall between the action just completed and the action forthcoming. Many critics have seen in these intermediate spaces evidence of Japanese aesthetic practices – Zen Buddhism, say, for Paul Schrader (see Kathe Geist, Chapter 4, this volume) and "pillow shots" for Noel Burch. Such spaces are sometimes called "still lifes" and, like the still lifes of classical painting, are often devoid of human figures. Ozu achieves a particular poignancy in many of his still lifes by highlighting the paradox of humanity's presence by its absence. Transitional spaces help viewers understand that a scene is changing and prepare them for the retrospective activity of reorienting themselves in the next scene. However, though transitional spaces help to indicate a change of scene or locale, it is not always clear where the new locale is until a later shot in the sequence (postponement of narrative information). And transitional spaces do little to help viewers understand how much time has passed. Here is an example of spatial change and temporal retrospectivity in *Tokyo Story*.

Between the first scene of the film, in which the older Hirayamas pack for their trip and discuss the stop in Osaka, and the second scene, which takes place in Koichi's house in Tokyo, there are three transitional spaces. The first is a shot of smokestacks (Figure 5). As Kathe Geist points out in Chapter 4, this is a recurring image of Tokyo in the film. It is not, however, an image unique to Tokyo and might as well be one of Osaka, Japan's commercial heartland. And since the film has prepared us for an Osaka outing, this may very well be our guess.[4] The next shot of power lines and a small railroad crossing (Figure 6) might be taken as representative of Tokyo, with its high energy and prominence in the postwar era. The following shot, however, makes it clear that we are in Tokyo, with its sign outside of Dr. Hirayama's office (Figure 7) (though we do not know that Koichi, the oldest child, is a doctor; in Ozu's films it is typically

FIGURE 5

difficult to follow familial relationships at first). Careful examination of the exterior shots in the rest of the film reveals that the smokestacks and train station are, in fact, spaces "connected" to Dr. Hirayama's, but nothing so indicates that at the start.

If we have, however, made the spatial transition from Onomichi to Tokyo, nothing in these intermediate spaces, these still lifes, has indicated any specific passage of time. For we find out shortly thereafter, though not before some small, seemingly irrelevant business about cleaning the house and asking a child to give up his room for his grandparents' visit, that not only has the film made the spatial transition from Onomichi to Tokyo, but so has the old couple. This is the ellipsis we discussed earlier, but we now understand that it occurred in the space and time of the intermediate shots.

This is not to say that Ozu handles all spatiotemporal changes in a deceptive or playful manner. For instance, when Ozu wants

FIGURE 6

to introduce the sequence in which Shukichi and Tomi stay over in Osaka when the latter takes ill, his intermediate spaces are clear and straightforward. The Osaka setting is established beyond a doubt by a shot of Osaka Castle, a massive stone structure instantly recognizable to virtually every Japanese. This is reinforced by a second shot of the Osaka skyline, this time with Osaka Castle in the background, a typical Ozu maneuver whereby the space of a scene is thoroughly explored by reverse angles and camera shifts. And it is to such strategies to which we now turn.

Ozu's scenic construction and segmenting of screen space are among the most notable characteristics of his cinema, yet casual viewers often fail to notice them. One of these is the frequency with which Ozu crosses the so-called 180-degree line. This crossing of the line results in what would be called in American film "mismatched" action within the same space. Characters who converse with each other seem to shift spatially in relation to each other and to the space in which they are filmed. Examples

FIGURE 7

from *Tokyo Story* abound. For instance, the first time we see the Hirayamas in the film, they are seated next to each other, each facing right (Figure 8). Yet by the time the sequence ends we suddenly notice that now they are facing left (Figure 9)! So bald a juxtaposition seems a bizarre mistake. One might explain it away in terms of the numerous angles and shots between the first time we see the couple and this last time at the end of the sequence. Numerous close-ups have been intercut, and cutaways to a neighbor lady have also occurred. Thus the precise moment of the shift from right to left may have passed us by.

More daring, yet more typical of Ozu, such apparent mismatches are not always disguised by cutaways but, in fact, represent a principle of cinematic spatial construction different from Hollywood's "norms." Critics have come to understand that Ozu uses a principle of 360-degree space instead of the 180-degree rule applied in Hollywood. For instance, in one of the most moving scenes of the film, in which the old mother tells her widowed daughter-in-law how much she enjoys her visit, the

FIGURE 8

FIGURE 9

daughter-in-law is initially screen right (Figure 10). Noriko gently massages Tomi's shoulders as they talk. Noriko then stands to move across the room (Figure 11). In the midst of her standing, Ozu cuts. In a typical American film this would be a cut on action, the action in some sense "disguising" the actual cut. Ozu cuts on her motion, too, but at the same time shifts the camera across the 180-degree line (Figure 12). Thus, when the cut on Noriko's motion is completed, she is now screen left.

In fact, the rest of this sequence, an important one in terms of its portrayal of loss, regret, and change, Ozu's camera traverses the entire space of the room, utilizing two-shots, close-ups, and reverse shots from every possible angle. Characters sitting side by side are typical in Ozu's cinema, reflective of the nonconfrontational stance of the Japanese, a certain politeness[5] (Figure 13). Notice here that Tomi, the mother-in-law, is facing screen left. When Ozu cuts to a close-up of her, however, she is facing screen right (Figure 14). Without the benefit of a cutaway this again appears to be a "mismatched action." And when Ozu returns to a two-shot (Figure 15), the screen direction does not correspond to the preceding shot, nor to the one before that (Figure 13). Careful examination of the individual setups reveals that Ozu rarely shoots a scene in a master shot, the whole scene or dramatic sequence done in one angle to which an editor can return periodically after using close-ups, reverse shots, over-the-shoulder shots, or other shots.

Changes in screen direction or seemingly mismatched action also occur regularly when Ozu shows continuous action across contiguous spaces. That is, when a character leaves one room of a house and enters another, Ozu does not typically imply spatial contiguity in the conventional way. Simply put, in a Hollywood film, when a character exits the frame to enter a contiguous space, screen direction hides the cut. If a character exits screen right, the next shot shows the character entering screen left. A smoothing out of the cut is thus made by the apparent continuity of motion left to right. Hollywood style and other variations on this classical continuity mode strive to achieve the *appearance*

FIGURE 10

FIGURE 11

FIGURE 12

of contiguity, whereas such sequences may have no basis in a
real space and time. (The Soviet theoretician and filmmaker Lev
Kuleshov convincingly proved this with regard to "creative geog-
raphy.") Hollywood filmmakers regard the cut as something to
be elided, to be made "invisible," and so principles of matching
screen direction and eyeline matches have been developed over
the years. As we have demonstrated, Ozu often disregards such
principles. Figures 32 and 33 (see Chapter 4 by Kathe Geist)
show this in action as Minoru exits one room of his house screen
right and enters the next frame, which is the next room, from
the same screen direction.

Attempting to account for these spatial anomalies can be difficult. Are they a cultural or an individual particularity? I am
convinced that a "cultural reading" of screen space in Ozu would
be reductive and essentialist, if not basically incorrect. I do think,
however, that Ozu has drawn inspiration for his spatialization
from aspects of traditional Japanese culture, including, most
prominently, architecture. The "mismatched" screen direction

FIGURE 13

FIGURE 14

FIGURE 15

in interior sequences (especially in houses) in which characters exit screen right and enter the next scene from the same direction may derive from the modularity of the Japanese home, in which space can be changed by the movement of sliding screens. Lower-level entryways that make a ring or border around the living area in a typical Japanese home provide a variety of entrances and exits into and out of rooms as well. Thus the space of the home itself can shift.[6] Combined with Ozu's proclivity for using individual setups for most shots, spatial configurations become important in individual scenes but much less so across the cut.

This is not to say that cutting, as such, is not important to Ozu, that the juxtaposition of shots to make meaning, to carry thematic weight, does not occur. There is a very shocking use of such a cut, in fact, in *Tokyo Story*. Tomi, playing with her youngest grandson, Isamu, muses over her fate and his. This, of course, is typical foreshadowing in which a character thinks about the future, cueing the audience to the possibility of the future being cut short. Though rare for Ozu (unlike other filmmakers), this is indeed what happens. But when Tomi muses about Isamu's future, wondering what will become of him, Ozu cuts to a shot of Shukichi, the grandfather, sitting alone. Is this a kind of "melodramatic" cut, Ozu implying that the same fate, of old age, loneliness, and disappointment, awaits Isamu? Yes and no.

Ozu has said that *Tokyo Story* was his "most melodramatic" film. Indeed, for critic Tony Rayns, Ozu may be taken at his word (see the review reprinted in this volume). The cut just described seems clearly to indicate that Isamu is doomed to a life like Shukichi's. But Ozu is too subtle a filmmaker, after all. Yes, Isamu may very well be doomed to such a life, but is such a life so bad? Or is there any alternative to such a life? Aging is inevitable, children grow up and grow apart from parents; that is to say, time brings changes. Yet there is also a cycle to life: birth, growth, death, the birth of a new generation and the pattern begins again. So if *Tokyo Story* is melodramatic in terms of its didacticism, teaching us to respect our elders, for instance, it is also realistic: life goes on no matter what one does. And in being so Japanese in terms of its historical setting and its familial characteristics, the film is also universal.

A ROUTINE PRODUCTION

Tokyo Story is only one of fourteen films Ozu made between 1948 and 1962. Oddly, this averages out to one film a year, a reminder of the vibrancy of the Japanese cinema in the 1950s, when directors routinely made a film each year, with many making as many as two or three. *Tokyo Story* was little different in its script preparation from most of Ozu's films. As was their habit, Ozu and co-writer Noda Kogo, with whom Ozu had worked for virtually his entire film career, went to an inn and hashed out the ideas over food, drink, and conversation. In this case, the inn was in Chigasaki and the script took 103 days to complete along with 43 bottles of sake.[7] Location scouting with Noda and cinematographer Atsuta Yuharu, script in hand, took a little less than one month, first in Tokyo, then in Onomichi. The film itself was shot and edited from July to October 1953. This four-month schedule is typical of Ozu: virtually all of his postwar films took four to five months to shoot and edit. There was no hint that *Tokyo Story* would surpass his other films in worldwide popularity and esteem.[8] In fact, it is arguable to say that *Tokyo Story* is his finest film, whatever one might mean by that. The point is, rather, that this film, made with the same crew Ozu had been using for years and featuring many of the same actors with whom he had worked so often before (Ryu Chishu had been in virtually every Ozu film since *Dragnet Girl* (*Hijosen no onna*) in 1933, was part of a routine, yet unique "project." With films spanning his career devoted to similar themes and with similar titles (the Japanese titles no less confusing than the English ones; "Tokyo" cropped up in four other films, for instance), Ozu played with variations on a theme. *Tokyo Story,* while it stands by itself as a masterpiece of world cinema, may also be taken as paradigmatic of Ozu's films, certainly his postwar films geared to the seemingly insular world of the Japanese middle-class family, yet speaking volumes about Japan as a whole and the world around.

The essays in this book were written with an eye to explaining specific characteristics of *Tokyo Story* and situating the film within Japanese culture, aesthetics, tradition, and history. In Chapter 1 Arthur Nolletti, Jr., examines the idea that *Tokyo Story* "borrows" from Leo McCarey's *Make Way for Tomorrow* (as, for instance, mentioned by Tony Rayns in the review reprinted in this volume). Nolletti's essay, the first attempt to consider this notion extensively, finds many points of similarity between the two films and discusses the significance of the differences.

Chapter 2 by Linda C. Ehrlich takes as its starting point the starting point of the film – the old couple's journey to visit their children in Tokyo. Ehrlich relates the journey to motifs of travel and pilgrimage in Japanese art, literature, and cinema. She highlights the genre of travel literature (*kiko*), along with *meisho-e* (pictures of famous places), *etoki* (traveling storytellers), and the final journey motif in noh and kabuki (*michiyuki*) to investigate how Ozu's film recollects aspects of Japanese tradition and makes them live in cinematic form.

Darell Davis, in Chapter 3, then explores, as the film does, the issue of the destination, Tokyo, and the dimensions that Tokyo occupies in the Japanese mind. His central conceit is that the mind-set of Tokyo was Ozu's maternal force as much as or more than his actual mother: Ozu as "Edokko," child of Tokyo. *Tokyo Story* examines the notion of a city as a parental force as it engages the question of the alliance of city and film against more traditional allegiances to family and kinship. This has implications for Ozu's vaunted "traditionalism" in which the hypertraditional style and characterization are a compensatory imagination of a reality that Ozu never had and urban Japanese have long lost.

In Chapter 4 Kathe Geist reviews the theories of empty space or "empty shots" in Ozu's films, illustrating each with examples from *Tokyo Story* and demonstrating that none excludes the others, but each is related to a different aspect of the film: formal, narrative, dramatic, and thematic. Japan's intertwined religious and aesthetic theories of space (*mu* and *ma*) are related to the persistent use of Buddhist symbols and artificats in the Onomichi sections of the film. Geist demonstrates that the empty spaces that some have seen as symptoms of "modernism" in Ozu have a long cultural history in Japanese religion and aesthetics.

Chapter 5 by Hasumi Shigekiho, perhaps the leading scholar and critic of Ozu in Japan, is a translated and revised portion of chapter 7 of his *Kantoku Ozu Yasujiro* (*Directed by Ozu Yasujiro*). Hasumi's essay is, on one level, an examination of the use of weather in Ozu's films but, on another, an analysis of the "Japaneseness" of Ozu. Hasumi makes the perhaps startling observation that the weather in Ozu's films seems always to be that of clear skies, and the heat his characters feel is not the oppressive humidity of midsummer, subtropical Japan, but rather the clear, dry air of southern California! Gone from Ozu's films is the rainy season; missing, too, are those seasonal markers in his other films – fallen leaves, plum blossoms, frost, so typical of haiku. His titles may speak of seasons, but his films almost cruelly ignore them. For this reason alone it is a mistake to regard Ozu as a "truly Japanese" film director. The death scene from *Tokyo Story* shows us that he is not a conservative director, nor a traditionalist, nor a truly Japanese director, but a flexible, open artist who can organize rich, multifaceted details with both unity and variety in his films. He is a citizen of the film republic, and just as Japan is different from what seems to be Japanese, his works might be better thought of as "Ozu-like."

NOTES

1. The name order in the essays in this volume is given in Japanese style, last name first, given name second.
2. The Japanese economic miracle, a theme that underlies *Tokyo Story* to some extent, was responsible, too, for making Japan the world's largest film producer; for instance, between 1957 and 1961 the Japanese averaged 500 feature films per year. Though a decline began in 1962, throughout the rest of the 1960s the Japanese averaged more than 350 films per year.
3. With an output of just over forty films, Ozu is far from being Japan's most prolific director. With directors like Inagaki and Misumi Kenji, who directed more than 100 films, and Makino Masahiro, who directed well over 200 films, Ozu's relatively scant output suggests that he was able to invest great care and effort into each film.
4. As if to illustrate the difference between Ozu's style and that of Hollywood, a 16-mm subtitled version of *Tokyo Story* available in the United States uses subtitles to identify the new location where no such indications are present!
5. Of course, one should be leery of such a sweeping cultural generalization. To converse, the Japanese naturally sit opposite each other, or at right angles, or obliquely, or many possible ways. Yet this "horizontality" not only is characteristic of Ozu but may be seen throughout the Japanese cinema. For instance, recall the many dinner scenes in *Family Game* (*Kazoku geemu*, Morita Yoshimitsu, 1984)

in which the family members are eating side by side, to great comic effect.

6. For a further discussion of this issue, consult my essay on Ozu's *Ohayo*, in "Childhood and Education in Japan," Teaching Module 3 (New York: The Japan Society, n.d.).

7. See Donald Richie, *Ozu* (Berkeley: University of California Press, 1974), 26.

8. Ozu's films received more *Kinema Jumpo* Best One awards than any other director (six), yet *Tokyo Story* did not win the Best One in 1953 (it was second).

I Ozu's *Tokyo Story* and the "Recasting" of McCarey's *Make Way for Tomorrow*

Critics have frequently observed that Ozu Yasujiro's *Tokyo monogatari* (*Tokyo Story,* 1953) was inspired by Leo McCarey's *Make Way for Tomorrow* (1937).[1] David Bordwell sees Ozu as "recasting" the American film – borrowing from it, adapting it – and briefly mentions that there are similarities in story, theme, and plot structure.[2] Indeed, these similarities are striking. Both films focus on an elderly couple who discover that their grown children regard them as a burden; both films are structured as

Make Way for Tomorrow (1937). Paramount. Producer and director: Leo McCarey. Screenplay: Viña Delmar, from the novel *The Years Are So Long* by Josephine Lawrence and the play of the same name by Helen and Nolan Leary. Photography: William C. Mellor. Special photographic effects: Gordon Jennings. Art direction: Hans Dreier and Bernard Herzbrun. Editing: LeRoy Stone. Music: Victor Young and George Antheil. Music director: Boris Morros. Sound: Walter Oberst and Don Johnson. Cast: Victor Moore (Barkley Cooper), Beulah Bondi (Lucy Cooper), Fay Bainter (Anita Cooper), Thomas Mitchell (George Cooper), Porter Hall (Harvey Chase), Barbara Read (Rhoda Cooper), Maurice Moscovitch (Max Rubens), Elisabeth Risdon (Cora Payne), Minna Gombell (Nellie Chase), Ray Mayer (Robert Cooper), Ralph Remley (Bill Payne), Louise Beavers (Mamie), Louis Jean Heydt (Doctor), Gene Morgan (Carlton Gorman), Gene Henning (Mr. Lockhart), Paul Stanton (Mr. Norton, hotel manager), Dell Henderson (Mr. Weldon, car salesman), Ruth Warren (secretary), Ferike Boros (Mrs. Rubens). 92 min.

journeys in which the couple are shuffled from one household to another; both films explore much of the same thematic material (e.g., sibling self-centeredness and parental disillusionment); and both films are about the human condition – the cyclical pattern of life with its concomitant joys and sorrows – and the immediate social realities that affect and shape that condition: in McCarey's film, the Great Depression; in Ozu's, the intensified postwar push toward industrialization. Primarily somber in tone but possessing rich and gentle humor, both films belong to a genre that in Japanese cinema is called the *shomin-geki,* films dealing with the everyday lives of the lower middle classes.[3]

Ozu never saw the McCarey film. But he did not really need to, since his scriptwriter, Noda Kogo, had and retained fond memories of it.[4] Furthermore, as a lifelong student of American film and as a director at Shochiku Studios, Ozu had firsthand knowledge of the American influence on Japanese film in general and the *shomin-geki* in particular. That influence, which began in the late teens with the popularity of Chaplin and Universal's now-forgotten "Bluebird movies," sentimental love stories focusing on rural life, took its most vital and concrete form in 1924 when Kido Shiro became manager at Shochiku's Kamata studio.[5] Kido established the *shomin-geki* as Shochiku's staple product and, along with it, American-style editing, a "one-bit-of-information-per-shot approach" that broke a scene down into static shots.[6] Working within this visual style, which he would later incorporate into his own, Ozu made his first of many films in the *shomin-geki* in 1929, *Kaisha-in seikatsu (The Life of an Office Worker).*[7] Of his films, none has received more critical acclaim or enjoyed greater popular success than *Tokyo Story.*

Building on Bordwell's suggestion that *Tokyo Story* recasts *Make Way for Tomorrow,* this essay will examine the relationship between the two films. First, I will explore three common connections: (1) the function and significance of the historical periods in which each film is set; (2) the special mood of laughter and tears; and (3) the duplication of specific scenes. Second, I will look at the two principal ways in which the films diverge: in visual style and in cultural values. In the end I hope to show not just the complex and often subtle give and take involved in the recasting process, but the way in which each film remains a separate and individual achievement. Before turning to an examination of the films' social and historical settings, however, I will briefly summarize the plots.

Adapted by Viña Delmar from Josephine Lawrence's novel, *The Years Are So Long* (1934), *Make Way for Tomorrow* focuses on the plight of Barkley and Lucy Cooper (Victor Moore and Beulah Bondi), a retired couple in their seventies who lose their family home because they cannot make the mortgage payments. When they turn to four of their five middle-aged children for financial help – the fifth never appears in the film – they are offered another option, which they accept with considerable misgivings: to separate temporarily until Nellie (Minna Gombell) and her husband (Porter Hall), the most prosperous members of the family, can take them both. Lucy will stay with George (Thomas Mitchell), the oldest son, his wife, Anita (Fay Bainter), and their teenage daughter, Rhoda (Barbara Read), in their Manhattan apartment, while Barkley will live with Cora (Elisabeth Risdon) and her unemployed husband, Bill (Ralph Remley), several hundred miles away. Neither arrangement works out, and when Nellie reneges on her promise, the couple's fate is sealed. Barkley will be sent to California to live with the fifth child, the never-seen Addie, presumably for his health; Lucy will go to a nursing home. Before the couple separate again, this time probably forever, they enjoy one last reunion. Deliberately passing up the farewell dinner prepared by the children, they visit the hotel where they honeymooned fifty years earlier. There they are treated with great kindness and generosity by the manager and staff, reminisce about their life, and enjoy themselves with a newfound freedom (Lucy even has an alcoholic drink). But eventually they must return to reality. At Grand Central Station, where Lucy sees Barkley off, they do their best to pretend that everything will be all right. As the train pulls away, Lucy takes one last look, then turns and walks away.

Tokyo Story concentrates on the Hirayamas, Shukichi (Ryu Chishu) and Tomi (Higashiyama Chieko), a retired elderly couple from the southern port town of Onomichi, who travel to Tokyo to visit their middle-aged children, their son Koichi (Yamamura So), a neighborhood doctor, and their daughter Shige (Sugimura Haruko), who runs a beauty shop in her home. (En route, they stop over in Osaka to see their youngest son, Keizo [Osaka Shiro], a visit that is only mentioned.) Although they are too gracious to admit it, even to themselves, their Tokyo visit turns out to be a disappointment because Koichi and Shige have little time for them. At one point, in order to get their parents out of the way, the two siblings even send them off to a spa (which caters to young people). When the couple make the mistake of returning to Shige's house earlier than expected, she turns them away. Only Noriko (Hara Setsuko), their widowed daughter-in-law, treats them with kindness and respect. Cutting their visit short, they decide to return home. But on the trip back, Tomi falls ill, forcing them to stop at Keizo's. Shortly after their arrival home, her condition worsens, and she dies. During the funeral, the family once again comes together, but soon afterward, Shige, Koichi, and Keizo return to their lives. Only Noriko stays behind to help Shukichi and Kyoko (Kagawa Kyoko), a schoolteacher and the one sibling still living with her parents. Before Noriko leaves, Shukichi thanks her for all she has done, gives her Tomi's watch as a keepsake, and releases her from any further obligation to him or the family. Alone, Shukichi contemplates the future.

As the plot summaries make clear, in both films the plight of the elderly and the dissolution of the family are intricately linked. What connects these two themes, what in part "explains" the callousness and selfishness of the couples' children, are the social and economic realities of the day. The characters in *Tokyo Story* never discuss Japan's postwar industrialization per se; nor do the characters in *Make Way for Tomorrow* ever utter the word

"Depression." Doing so was unnecessary, since audiences knew about these conditions from their own lives.

Produced by Paramount in 1936, during the Depression, *Make Way for Tomorrow* was an anomaly: a serious American film about old age that made few, if any, concessions to the box office. Adolph Zukor, then president of the studio and a supporter of the film and frequent visitor to the set, urged McCarey to make the ending happier, but to no avail.[8] When the film was released in 1937, it proved a commercial failure (but a critical success). Paramount, which had been hit hard by the Depression – it suffered bankruptcy in 1933 and underwent court-ordered reorganization until 1935[9] – now had a new president: Barney Balaban. McCarey was fired.

Barkley Cooper's plight in *Make Way for Tomorrow* is one that was shared by millions of Americans. A retired bookkeeper, he has not worked for four years, having left his job or lost it in 1932 or 1933 at the height of the Depression. Throughout the film, he tries his best to find a new job, not in order to save his house, which is beyond saving, but to reunite with Lucy and regain a measure of his dignity and independence. But as Rhoda, their granddaughter, tells Lucy in the only moment in which she offers sympathy and understanding, "Why kid yourself, Grandma? You know he can't get a job. He's much too old." That the system not only lets the Coopers down but also discriminates against them is made painfully evident on several occasions. During one of the most poignant, Barkley sees a sign in a clothing store window for a clerking job and excuses himself from Lucy to go inside to apply. McCarey, with great tact, keeps the viewer outside with Lucy. She knows exactly what Barkley is doing, and when he returns, offering the excuse "They didn't have anything in my size," she pretends to accept it in order to save his pride. Moments later, the couple see another sign in another store window. "Save while you're young," it urges. "Fine time to tell us," Barkley says dryly.

To help people like the Coopers, Roosevelt's New Deal of 1934 and 1935 pushed hard for reform legislation. Among the most important was the Social Security Act of August 1935, which provided two types of assistance for the aged. Those who were destitute could receive federal aid of up to fifteen dollars per month, depending on matching sums provided by the states; those who were working could receive, upon retirement, annuities provided from taxes on their earnings and their employer's payroll. The Act also provided for unemployment insurance. Theoretically, Barkley was eligible for assistance, but in actuality, Social Security could not help those already unemployed in 1935. Therefore, in April of that same year, Congress voted to provide work relief with the Works Progress Administration, which enrolled more than 2 million workers between 1935 and 1941 on a wide variety of projects, mostly in public works and conservation.[10] But like many Americans, Barkley Cooper still fell through the cracks.

In *Tokyo Story* Hirayama Shukichi is a retired head of a board of education, but unlike the Coopers, he and Tomi never find themselves in dire economic straits. Rather, their loss is emotional and personal. Yet this is not to suggest that the Hirayamas' situation and suffering are any the less painful. Indeed, they too are caught up in a massive historical upheaval, for 1953, the year the film was made and the time in which it is set, lies roughly midway between the revision of the Civil Code of 1948 (which supplanted the Meiji Civil Code of 1898) and the beginning of Japan's rapid economic growth, a process that the film shows to be already under way.

The Meiji Civil Code of 1898, which was family-centered, served Japan when it had an agrarian-based economy.[11] In this prewar economy the prevalent family system was the "stem family," consisting of a married couple, the couple's unmarried children, the couple's eldest son, and his wife and children – in short, a three-generation family. Parents and children had status based on economics since they were part of the family, and productive members at that. It was a unique cultural tradition that was strengthened by such Confucian precepts as filial obligation, which privileged the elderly.

The Civil Code of 1948 served to codify a lifestyle patterned after a Western capitalist and democratic model. It did away with primogeniture inheritance and stressed a philosophy of individual rights, namely the dignity of the individual, equality of the sexes, and high regard for offspring. In so doing, it recognized that the urbanization and industrialization that had occurred in Japan since the war had dramatically affected the family structure and relationships. Put simply, family members more often than not were now working outside the family unit and even began moving away from their hometown. This geographical mobility, which went hand in hand with industrialization, served to weaken the family. But what undermined the family even more was the philosophy accompanying industrialization and modern capitalism, the "idea of success, individualism, and what might be called 'the wish to be free.' "[12] It is this philosophy that is embraced by the middle-aged children in both films.

It is ironic that while McCarey's film deals with a time of great economic hardship and Ozu's with a time of emerging economic prosperity, the effect on both families is devastating.

In the opening scene of *Make Way for Tomorrow,* it quickly becomes apparent that the Coopers' children have no intention of coming to their parents' rescue by helping them financially. George, acting as his brother and sisters' spokesman, spells out the reasons why such help is out of the question: Nellie would say that her husband's business has never been worse; Cora would explain that her husband is out of work and that she herself may have to get a job; Addie lives too far away; Robert is – well, Robert is Robert (implying that he is unreliable); and as for himself, he and Anita have Rhoda's college to think about (Figure 16). Therefore, the children decide that the best solution is for Lucy and Barkley to live with George and Cora, respectively. They do not reach this decision, however, without squabbling among themselves – Robert accuses Nellie of having plenty

FIGURE 16

of money – and resorting to one-upmanship – Nellie promises to do more for her parents eventually than either George or Cora. The parents, meanwhile, are bemused and confused (Figure 17).

Wholly preoccupied with their own bourgeois aspirations, the Cooper children offer help to their parents only grudgingly. And although they do not realize it, they are victims of these aspirations. Thus Nellie pays for her life in a gilded cage by being married to a boor. She may wear fur-lined satin dressing gowns, sport platinum blonde hair like Jean Harlow, and lead an active social life, but she has no say in her marriage and would not be permitted to take her mother for one evening, even if she wanted to. Therefore, it comes as no surprise when she reneges on her promise to take in both of her parents. Though George and Anita try to do better by his parents, and in some ways do, in the end they too fail. In fact, it is George, the most sensitive and caring of the children, who sends his mother to an old-age

FIGURE 17

home because she cannot "fit in." Finally, there is Cora. Sharp-featured and dour, she tries to create the impression that she is patient, mild-mannered, and put-upon, but in reality she is angry and frustrated. The least well off of the children, she lives in a small, drab bungalow, speaks with a flat Midwestern accent (unlike Anita and Nellie, who sound like dowagers), and has no time for amenities like treating her father kindly. As we shall see, she may even have served in part as the model for Shige, for the two characters have much in common.

The children in *Tokyo Story* treat their parents no better than do their American counterparts. The very fact that the Hiraya-mas must travel to see them rather than vice versa is indicative of the profound social changes taking place in Japan and the bourgeois aspirations that drive Shige and Koichi. All their time, energy, and thought are devoted to running their businesses, concentrating on their immediate (nuclear) families, and living their own lives – in short, adhering to "the wish to be free." They fail to see that the real purpose of their parents' visit is not to vacation or sightsee but to shore up weakened family ties. Yet what becomes disturbingly clear is that Shige and Koichi no longer feel pressing emotional ties to their parents. Nor for that matter does Keizo, though, to his credit, he experiences one moment of genuine grief and regret at his mother's funeral. In place of natural feeling, all three can only offer filial obligation, albeit of a very limited kind. Thus when Koichi is forced to cancel a Sunday outing that he plans for his parents because a patient requires his attention – something, of course, for which he cannot be blamed – he sees no need to make it up to them or spend more time with them. Shige is even more ungiving. In fact, she is downright stingy. She "treats" her parents to inexpensive crackers, eats the expensive cake that her husband buys them (after scolding him for spending the money in the first place), and tells her brother that sukiyaki (rather than sukiyaki and sashimi) is good enough for their parents' first dinner in Tokyo. Like the children in McCarey's film, Shige, Koichi, and Keizo slight their parents not because they are cruel but because they are thoughtless. And while both sets of children obviously have been coarsened by harsh reality and the need to "get ahead" (*risshin shusse*), ultimately their behavior must be attributed to one thing only: their own deficient characters.

A second connection between *Tokyo Story* and *Make Way for Tomorrow* is the films' shared mood, the mixture of laughter and tears. It is this mood, in fact, that is primarily responsible for the *shomin-geki*'s most distinctive feature: its depiction of life's difficulties with warmth, humor, sympathy, and compassion. Leo McCarey once remarked, "I like people to laugh, I like people to cry."[13] In so doing, he was speaking about the *shomin-geki*, although he probably had never heard of the Japanese genre. And when he made *Make Way for Tomorrow*, he was in essence making a *shomin-geki* and using laughter and tears in many of the same ways that Ozu did throughout his career: to capture life in its purest and most essential form, to temper what otherwise would be too bleak and painful to bear, to show that life could be "at once hysterically funny and pungently sad."[14]

On the whole, both films find their mixture of laughter and tears in gentle humor. Take, for example, the scene in *Make Way for Tomorrow* with Lucy's squeaking rocking chair. The squeaking is music to Lucy's ears, a comforting sound that accompanies the lulling rhythm of the rocking itself. For her it evokes hearth and home. But when she and her chair are plopped down in the middle of George and Anita's living room, which happens to be filled with Anita's bridge students (middle-aged couples dressed inexplicably in formal attire), she proves not just a distraction but a social embarrassment. Warned by George and Anita's glances, she stops rocking but soon – and quite unintentionally – finds a new way to be a distraction and social embarrassment: by kibitzing with the students. The scene is funny and heartrending at the same time, for we realize that while Lucy is simply trying to fit in, her squeaking rocker and kibitzing have exactly the opposite effect. We also realize that, trivial though Lucy's "offenses" may be, they quickly add up and become the greatest source of irritation between her and George's family.[15] And in the end it is Lucy who suffers most.

In *Tokyo Story* gentle humor is introduced in the opening sequence as Shukichi and Tomi, seated side by side, pack for their trip. At one point Tomi asks Shukichi if he has their air pillow in his bag; he claims that he gave it to her to pack. Both then begin looking through their belongings. Briefly interrupted by a neighbor lady, who stops by to wish them a bon voyage, they resume their search, until Shukichi says, "I've found it," to which Tomi replies, "You've found it, have you?" As Keiko McDonald rightly points out, this incident illuminates their characters, showing us "a conjugal happiness that has lasted into old age" and a "harmony within themselves and with the external world."[16] This incident also shows them to be very human. Shukichi, after practically blaming Tomi for misplacing the item, doubtless knows that if anyone deserves blame, it is he. But he neither admits guilt nor offers an apology. At least not in so many words. Nevertheless, he realizes, and she does too, that his admission, "I've found it," is an apology in itself, since it is spoken in the knowledge that he has been forgetful, that he has been wrong. Tomi, of course, understands all of this and "forgives" him: "You've found it, have you?" Nothing else need be said.

Occasionally, the gentle humor in both films gives way to broad humor. The best example in each film is a scene in which the father is bullied and berated by his most vinegary daughter. In *Make Way for Tomorrow* Barkley, suffering from a bad cold, refuses to cooperate with the young doctor (Louis Jean Heydt) making the house call, much to Cora's irritation and embarrassment. As the scene opens, Barkley is lying on the living room couch, where he sleeps, trading jabs with Cora. "Your mother'd get me on my feet so quick it would make your head spin," he says. But she only pooh-poohs him: "You've only got a little cold." When the doctor arrives early, Cora literally pulls Barkley from the couch and rushes him into Bill's and her bed. She means to look the part of the dutiful daughter. But Barkley behaves like a recalcitrant child in order to expose her and get even with her. He even ends up biting the doctor. Having had enough, Cora forgets about appearances and scolds her father. "What's the matter with you?" she asks, towering over him.

In the equivalent scene in *Tokyo Story* a staggeringly drunken Shukichi and two equally drunken friends are brought to Shige's late at night by the police. Nearly comatose, Shukichi collapses into one of the beauty parlor chairs, while Shige paces around him, whining and complaining and at one point even shoving him, pulling his hat off his head and plopping it unceremoniously back down again. What makes the scene especially funny is not just that Shukichi has temporarily cast aside his patriarchal dignity and let off a little steam, but that he has – albeit unintentionally – discomforted, inconvenienced, embarrassed, and angered Shige, who of course deserves such treatment. "I never dreamed he'd come back here tonight, even if he'd been alone," she says in disgust, referring to the fact that earlier that day she had thrown her parents out. Like Cora, she has no sympathy for or understanding of her father; nor can she see herself for what she really is. Such cruelty and blindness perhaps deserve broad humor and sweet revenge. Still, the humor is qualified by a sense of pathos, a lingering sadness in the fact that the father–daughter relationship has come to this.

Both *Tokyo Story* and *Make Way for Tomorrow* are characterized by a gradation of moods that range from the comic to the serious and somber. In fact, Ozu described *Tokyo Story* as "one of my most melodramatic pictures," a comment that has puzzled many critics. Tony Rayns claims that the film's melodrama may well be an example of the influence of McCarey's film, especially since much of the melodrama in both films derives from the explicit, almost didactic, handling of thematic material.[17] Although Rayns seems to forget that melodrama and didacticism were nothing new to Ozu – for example, they played a prominent role in the *shomin-geki* / salaryman comedy *Umarete wa mita keredo* (*I was Born, But . . .* , 1932)[18] – his claim has genuine merit. *Tokyo Story* has more plot and more "drama" than many of Ozu's late films; the film's central event is Tomi's death (though, to be sure, Ozu treats it with characteristic restraint and utmost solemnity); and there are "explicit discussions of piety, kindness, and the nature of life,"[19] along with the underscoring of the film's themes by the proverbs "Be good to your parents while they are alive" and "No one can serve his parents beyond the grave." That *Make Way for Tomorrow* crystallizes its theme in much the same way should come as no surprise. An opening title card enjoins us to "honor thy father and mother."

The final connection between the two films has to do with "duplication," that is, the ways in which Ozu's film mirrors, borrows from, and reworks McCarey's. I have already discussed a fair number of these, such as the films' themes, the characters of Cora and Shige, and the mood of laughter and tears. Now I will consider two sets of scenes in which the duplications are unusually striking, and then will briefly look at several notable parallels in character, function, and theme that have not yet been mentioned.

In the first set of scenes Barkley and Shukichi openly express their disappointment in their children. They do so reluctantly, and even try to make excuses for them. Barkley, for example, no sooner greets his storekeeper-friend, Mr. Rubens (Maurice Moscovitch), than he protests, without much conviction, "I hope I didn't give you the wrong impression about Cora. She's a fine girl." He quickly follows this with "It's nice to live with your children" and "All-in-all, my children are very fine." But Mr. Rubens knows exactly how Cora treats Barkley, for – alas – he has children of his own. In his view both Barkley and he are foolish, long-suffering fathers, in his word, *schlemiels*. Perhaps not surprisingly, when Barkley tries to use the word, he ends up getting it all wrong. Like Barkley, Shukichi would like to think the best of his children. Thus, while well on his way to getting drunk with his friends, Mr. Numata (Tono Eijiro) and Mr. Hattori (Nagaoka Teruko), he explains: "We can't expect too much from our children. Times have changed and we have to face it." The pain and disillusionment that the two patriarchs feel is palpable, and it is interesting that in both scenes the people they have chosen to confide in are men like themselves, disappointed fathers.

The more the men talk, the closer they get to the core of their disappointment. For Mr. Numata, everything comes down to the terrible neglect that he feels: "He [my son] never pays any attention to me." For Mr. Rubens, what hurts most is his children's lack of respect and natural feelings: "When they get older, and you can't give them as much as other children, they are ashamed of you. And when you give them everything and put them through college, they're ashamed of you." For Shukichi and Barkley, nothing is worse than the sense of loss. "My son has really changed, but it can't be helped," Shukichi admits. Then, once again protecting his children, he quickly adds, "There really are too many people in Tokyo." Barkley, remembering the closeness and affection he and his children once shared, says, "You know, I sometimes think that children should never grow past the age where you have to tuck them into bed at night."

If there is a fundamental difference between these Japanese and American fathers, it is in the way they express themselves, the tone they take. Barkley's comment about lost closeness is tinged with bitterness; Mr. Rubens's comment – "I'm proud of my children. They don't need me and I don't need them" – is steeped in it. Of the Japanese, only Mr. Numata seems to give in to bitterness when he says, "Nowadays some young people would kill their parents without a single thought. Mine at least wouldn't do that." His comment, though far from being bitter – or even sarcastic – is in actuality an oblique example of Japanese modesty. Mr. Numata loves his son and is saying that, in spite of everything, his son probably loves him too. And that "probably" is reason enough to be proud, at least in the early hours of the morning when one has had too much to drink. In short, these two scenes have a great deal in common. Indeed, scriptwriter Noda seems to have had in mind not just the McCarey scene but also its most salient details.

The second set of scenes deals with the same subject – parental disillusionment – only now Shukichi and Barkley are speaking with their wives, and all are trying to console themselves. For both couples, this is a rare opportunity and comes at a time when they are by themselves and free from the obligations and routines of daily life. Barkley and Lucy are spending their last five hours before his train leaves for California; Tomi and Shukichi are relaxing at Keizo's boardinghouse, where Tomi is recovering after having taken ill on the train. As might be expected, what weigh heavily on their minds are their children. But out of respect for each other's feelings, they proceed indirectly, cautiously. Barkley blames himself for the untenable situation that he has put Lucy, himself, and even the children in. "I was a failure," he says, meaning that if he had succeeded in the business world, things would be different. But Lucy insists that he is no failure; then, speaking directly about the children, she says,

"I tried always to be a good mother. But if I'd been all that I thought I was, things would be different now. You don't sow wheat and reap ashes." She knows what their children are, but cannot bring herself to criticize them, so she blames herself. Shukichi and Tomi do not wish to admit the truth about their children either, yet little by little, they do. Shukichi comments that Shige "used to be much nicer," and by way of agreement, Tomi adds, "Koichi's changed too. He used to be such a nice boy." Finally, Shukichi admits the most painful truth of all: that their children not only haven't lived up to expectations but are greedy into the bargain. The couple share a knowing smile, but it is not in their nature to be ungenerous or self-pitying. Therefore, contradicting themselves, they claim that their children are better than most and that they themselves are lucky. Likewise, Barkley and Lucy try to put things in the best possible light, and while they do not contradict themselves, they do in effect end up saying that they are lucky. After all, if as Lucy says, "people are entitled to just so much happiness in life," then they cannot complain, because they have certainly had their portion. Both scenes end in much the same way, with the couples reaffirming once more what can never be taken from them or compromised: their conjugal harmony and solidarity.

To be sure, there are many other examples of duplication, some more important than others. Here we will briefly comment on three. First, there is the function of the grandchildren. Both Minoru and Rhoda resent their grandparents because their presence in the house is an inconvenience: the former has to give up his study; the latter has to share her bedroom with Lucy. Neither grandchild makes much effort to get to know the grandparents, though Rhoda – no doubt because she is older than Minoru – at least has some minimal interest in Lucy. Second, there is Keizo and George's painful recognition that they have betrayed their parents. Keizo comes to this realization at his mother's funeral; George does so immediately after sending his mother to a nursing home. Looking at himself in a mirror, he tells Anita, "As the years go by, you can be mighty proud of me." Third, and most important, there is the motif of separation. For the elderly couples nothing is more terrifying than the prospect of parting. Yet this is exactly what happens, though separation takes two very different forms: death in *Tokyo Story*, living apart in *Make Way*. In both films, it is the women who verbalize this fear. Early on, Lucy tries to tell her children, "Your father and I thought that no matter what happened, we'd always be –." But feeling that they would neither understand nor be interested in her sentiments, she simply says, "Oh, never mind what we thought." Tomi, on her way to an overnight stay at Noriko's after she and Shukichi have been thrown out of Shige's, finds herself separated from her husband for the first time in their marriage. The experience is even more distressing because they are on their own in a large and unfamiliar city. "If we got lost," Tomi says to Shukichi, trying to mask her fear, "we might never find each other again." This moment is given added poignancy by Ozu's use of a long shot, which shows the couple to be out of place in their surroundings.[20] It is the lowest point of their visit.

In this last part of the essay, I will focus on the two most important points of divergence in the films: cinematic style and cultural values. With respect to style, no one – not even McCarey's most ardent supporters – would suggest that his film had any influence whatever on Ozu's. Quite simply one of cinema's greatest directors, Ozu is revered for his minimalist and restrained style. That style – with its predominantly stationary camera; deliberate, meditative tempo; unusually low camera position ("tatami shots"); full, frontal shots of speakers; transitional shots of seemingly unrelated settings ("pillow shots"); and narrative symmetries, parallels, and ellipses – is highly personal and immediately recognizable, and has been thoroughly studied.[21] McCarey's style, in contrast, conforms to the editing codes of classical Hollywood cinema and has been described as "anonymous" and "sometimes awkward."[22] Yet even those critics who find McCarey most deficient in style and technical artistry praise him for certain scenes in *Make Way for Tomorrow* in which "he achieves and then explores an emotional and spiritual depth that one might ordinarily find only in a Mizoguchi, an Ozu or a Bresson."[23] This is high praise, indeed, and as it turns out, not unwarranted.

Two scenes that critics invariably single out for such praise are Lucy's long-distance phone conversation with Barkley, which interrupts Anita's bridge class, and George's having to break the news to Lucy that she must go to a nursing home. In these scenes, McCarey's style goes beyond the merely functional and becomes truly expressive. As Charles Affron says of the first scene, "Merely a succession of conventionally framed shots, first of an old woman's back and then of her face, is sufficient to involve us in an affect compounded of guilt and embarrassment at seeing that face, the face of the mother we can never love enough."[24] During the first part of the phone call, with her back turned to the bridge players and camera alike, and speaking just a little too loudly, Lucy voices her love and loneliness, much to the discomfort and irritation of the assembled company. As the conversation continues, McCarey cuts to a shot of Lucy's face. In the background we see the players – "our in-frame surrogates."[25] As she gently chides Barkley for spending money on a phone call instead of a much-needed winter scarf, "then goes on to say how good the children are to her, how nice their guests are and how much she misses him and wants to be with him again," the faces of these listeners gradually soften to sympathy.[26] Here McCarey's simple and unadorned style enables us to see even more than our in-frame surrogates. By doing so, it achieves an understatement, sublimity, and authenticity of feeling that make up for his sometimes blunt and heavy-handed direction elsewhere.

The second scene is even more moving and effective. Here both George and his mother face a terrible, virtually impossible task. Against his will, and much to his shame, he must inform her that he is sending her to a nursing home. She, of course, already knows, having seen a letter from the nursing home and having just exchanged half-hidden glances with him as he prepares to speak. What gives the scene power, along with the writing and acting, is McCarey's use of space and high- and low-angle shots. As James Harvey says, "McCarey has kept mother and son each in their separate spheres of distress, cutting between shots."[27] From a high angle, representing George's point of view, the camera looks down at Lucy, who is seated in her rocker. Her point of view of him is represented by a low angle, in which he is seen as a towering but slumped figure – that is, a man who is burdened by having to do something he hates. To save him from his shame and to salvage her own pride, she pretends that it is her idea to go to the nursing home, that in fact she *wants* to go. Each knows, of course, exactly what is happening, that this conversation is really a matter of form, but McCarey makes us feel that it is "through this sort of tact, taste, discretion that affection somehow survives – even scenes like this one."[28] Their conversation finished, a decision having been agreed upon, McCarey now includes mother and son in the same shot (and space) for the last time in the film. Touching his face, she confides to him, "And here's another little secret, just between you and me. You were always my favorite child." He embraces her, and she pats him on the shoulder, as if to comfort him. It is a shattering moment, for it is deeply touching and deeply ambiguous.

To be sure, McCarey cannot equal Ozu, even in the two scenes just described, but in the ambiguity and understatement, in leaving something unsaid, he uses his simple and spare classical Hollywood style to good effect and, as in the *shomin-geki* at its best, captures the nature and integrity of common people.

Finally, let us look at the closing scenes of both films, examining the cultural values they embody. The lengthy climactic sequence of *Make Way for Tomorrow,* in which Barkley and Lucy spend what is probably their last time together, leaves realism behind. Rich in sentiment and humor, this sequence is easy to criticize as Hollywood fantasy, but it is "a perfect, magical moment during which time is suspended, the past recaptured, the present sorrow annihilated, with the outside world unobtrusively and faultlessly joining in the celebration."[29] Like the ending of Murnau's *Der Letzte Mann* (*The Last Laugh,* 1924) and the couple's visit to the city in his *Sunrise* (1927), this sequence in McCarey's film is healing and restorative, a vision of what life should be.

In this sequence Barkley and Lucy finally receive the generous treatment and respect they deserve. A car salesman (Dell Henderson), at first intent only on making a sale, offers them a demonstration ride, but when he learns that they aren't interested in buying a car, he is not in the least angry or irritated. In fact, in this best of all possible worlds, he takes Barkley and Lucy to the hotel where they spent their honeymoon. A checkroom girl takes time to talk with them and, learning about their visit fifty years ago, introduces them to the manager (Paul Stanton). He not only speaks with them, but invites them to be guests of the hotel for the evening. Even the hotel's orchestra leader is unfailingly considerate. Seeing that Barkley and Lucy are not quite able to manage a fast dance, he plays a waltz for them, "Let Me Call You Sweetheart," which just happens to be "their song."

In virtually every way the sequence represents release from quotidian reality at its most drab and oppressive. Gone are the confinement and grayness of Cora's house and George and Anita's apartment. The Manhattan of these scenes – the posh East Side – is a place of pure splendor and luxury, and is filled with smartly dressed people who seem never to have heard of the Depression. At one point, in one of his most expansive moving-camera shots in the film, McCarey pans across the hotel's spacious lobby, which has been greatly enlarged and expensively refurbished since the couple's original visit. Thus the hotel is both the same and different. In its newly acquired opulence, it can be seen as symptomatic of the materialism that impels society, including the Coopers' children, and helps make couples like the Coopers obsolete. Aware of this irony, McCarey makes it a point to show that the hotel has not forgotten its past or tossed it aside. On the contrary, it proudly retains it by keeping on display a photo of the lobby as it was fifty years ago. The hotel thus functions as the ideal America, just as the kindly staff functions as the ideal children – and ideal audience surrogate.

In this privileged world, Barkley and Lucy finally get the chance to show – and be appreciated for – their intelligence, wit, and warmheartedness, their knowledge of what is important in life and how to take pleasure in it. Even more significantly, Barkley comes to the realization that the only things that matter are Lucy and himself and rediscovering the relationship they had "before they became absorbed into the norms of democratic-capitalist domesticity."[30] He, therefore, informs her that they will not go to the children's farewell dinner for them. When Lucy protests that they cannot just skip it, Barkley asks, "Why not?" Robin Wood has called Barkley's question "the ultimate anarchic question."[31] It is also a quintessentially American question: what it stands for is the championing of individuality and the repudiation of anything that threatens or tries to destroy that individuality. Barkley, in short, takes a stand, asserting his and Lucy's right to do what they wish and be who they are. Treating society and his children as oppressors, he defies the former for denying him a chance to work and the latter for betraying the natural bond between parents and children – a bond that has proved illusory. Barkley's gesture of defiance is a veritable pox on both your houses, but it also amounts to a reaffirmation of self, for it implies that one need not have a place within the economy to have individual worth, that, in fact, one's essential self and one's role in society are two entirely different things. It is this realization that leads Barkley to address Lucy by her maiden name, Miss Breckenridge, when he says his last good-bye to her. "Mother," even "wife," is a role; "Miss Breckenridge," on the other hand, signifies the essential self – the woman – just as "Barkley Cooper" signifies the essential self, the man. This is the only relationship – man and woman simply together – that Barkley deems valid.

Although one might call Barkley's position "anarchic" since it disengages Lucy and himself from all familial and social obligations, in actuality it is American to the core in its upholding of individualism in the face of authority. It also allows Barkley a unique moment of bravado. Phoning Nellie, he tells her in no uncertain terms – and in apparently strong language that we do not hear but can easily imagine – that Lucy and he will not be coming for dinner. Nellie is speechless. With this phone call, the "fantasy" element of the sequence reaches its climax. Barkley has had the satisfaction of telling his children off, and the audience has been assured that there is still some justice in the world. The film, however, isn't simply interested in settling the score; it means to punish, too. Thus the Cooper children aren't just rotten; they must be made to know that their parents know they are rotten.

However gratifying this moment may be, it is at best a Pyrrhic victory, for in the end nothing has changed. Barkley goes off to California, and Lucy goes off to the nursing home (though doubtless she will first have some explaining to do to her fractious, insulted brood). McCarey does not want us to see matters quite this way. Nor does he want us to think about the implications of Barkley's renunciation of family and society or the fact that, philosophically, the couple are left to their own resources and must make a virtue of necessity, since society has no comfort or consolation to offer. What McCarey means for us to see instead is that Barkley and Lucy have managed to preserve what is theirs and only theirs, and that this can never be taken away. It is a lovely sentiment, and it produces an admittedly moving and bittersweet finale. But as a philosophic position, it is ultimately wanting. Dealing, as it does, exclusively with the personal, the self, it fails to address the many questions that the Coopers' plight raises.

The closing scenes of *Tokyo Story* provide a marked contrast to those of *Make Way for Tomorrow*. There is no sequence of happiness and make-believe, no settling the score with the bad children, or even confronting them, and thus they remain free to believe that they have done well by their parents. Nor does Ozu alter his style. Indeed, there is no need to, for though Tomi has died, Ozu shows that life goes on, which is to say that he shows life, as he always does, in all its ordinariness, beauty, and sadness. For Ozu, one of the inalienable truths about life is that it is ephemeral and that in this ephemerality lies an inherent sadness, what the Japanese call *mono no aware*. In the face of such a truth, one must find a way to make the pain and suffering of life somehow bearable. This is not easy under any circumstances, but it is impossible if one is dedicated only or chiefly to the self. And here is where Western and Japanese views of life differ most profoundly.

As some critics have pointed out, in the film's last scenes, Shukichi, Noriko, and Kyoko – the three most selfless characters – find a faith or philosophy that helps them come to terms with their sadness and disappointment.[32] In the first of these scenes, Noriko speaks with Kyoko, who cannot understand her brothers' and sisters' lack of family feelings. "They are selfish," she declares bluntly. Noriko knows exactly how Kyoko feels, but she does a rather strange thing: she defends the brothers and sisters. "Children do drift away," she explains, adding that they meant no harm. Here we see an all-important difference between the two women. Kyoko, who is still young and idealistic, fails to recognize that time itself can weaken family ties. Not only does Noriko know this, but as she confides to Kyoko, she fears that in time she may change too, in spite of herself. "Isn't life disappointing?" Kyoko wonders. Noriko quietly agrees: "Yes, it is." The two women can go no further than this: for them life is filled with pathos, sadness, and tears.

Only one character goes beyond this view of life: Shukichi. Possessing an inner strength and wisdom, he manages in the days following Tomi's death to move beyond grief. We see this for the first time in the penultimate scene, in which he bids Noriko good-bye. Setting aside formality to speak openly and affectionately, he tells her that he is sincerely concerned about her future. "I want you to be happy. I really mean it," he says. Urging her to remarry and thanking her for the kindness she has shown Tomi and him, he repeatedly tells her that she is "truly a good woman," even when she denies it and unexpectedly bursts into tears. As the conversation comes to a close, he gives her Tomi's watch as a memento. Its full significance, however, does not become clear until the next scene, when we see Noriko on the train that is taking her back to Tokyo and out of Shukichi's life. A look of calm on her face, she removes the watch from her purse and holds it thoughtfully. This is not merely a sentimental gesture, but, according to Keiko McDonald, an indication that she has undergone a change, that she will allow time to pass of its own accord.[33] Thus Shukichi has given her the most precious gift of all: he has helped her begin the journey in search of calm acceptance and serenity.

In the final scene, in which we return to the Hirayama household, we see that Shukichi has successfully made this journey, that he has attained a gentle serenity and resigned acceptance. A companion to the opening scene in which Shukichi and Tomi were seated side by side, packing for their trip, this scene employs the same camera setup (Tomi's presence is marked by an empty space), offers a variation on the same basic story material (the exchange of familiar, everyday commonplaces), and includes the same next-door neighbor. Thus the scene suggests the cyclic nature of life. As it opens, Shukichi is fanning himself and looking out at the sea. A few moments pass; then he is greeted by his neighbor. "Everyone's gone now. You'll be lonely then," she says cheerfully. Far from being an insensitive comment, her greeting touches the very center of his being, giving voice to his thoughts and reality. He is pleased, he is grateful, he understands. "If I had known things would come to this," he says, "I'd have been kinder to her." His statement is both an admission of past shortcomings and a serene acceptance of what life brings, and it reminds us of how different he is now and how far he has journeyed since he uttered his stunned expression of grief upon learning of Tomi's imminent death: "So . . . this is the end, then." After a few more amenities are exchanged, the neighbor leaves, and Shukichi returns to looking out at the sea. Now he is silent. Now he is left to carry on alone, but in his self-control and stoicism he is at one with his world. As Paul Schrader says, what Shukichi has come to accept is this: "There exists a deep ground of compassion and awareness, which man and nature can touch intermittently. This, of course, is the Transcendental."[34] A philosophy of quiet resignation, it is also quintessentially Japanese, and worlds removed from the notion of individualism espoused in *Make Way for Tomorrow*.

In closing, let us imagine a scene that might have taken place between Ozu and Noda, director and scriptwriter, lifelong friends and companions. About to begin the arduous work of creating a script, they go to an inn, as they have often done before – perhaps the same inn where Shukichi and Tomi stayed in *Tokyo Story*. There, as they have also done many times before, they stay up late, talking, sharing ideas, agreeing, disagreeing, and drinking sake – many bottles of sake.[35] Noda has already told Ozu about an American film he saw and loved concerning an elderly couple and their children, and now Ozu and he are there to make it their own. Even if this scene did not happen in quite this way, one thing remains certain: the parallels, similarities, and common connections between Ozu's and McCarey's films are not only numerous, but pervasive and involve character, theme, tone, dialogue, and dramatic situation. Indeed, even when the two films diverge, there is always some point of contact and connection, no matter how small it may be. To be sure, the presence of similarities does not in itself prove that Ozu borrowed from McCarey's film in every case. And the simple truth is that we will never know for sure the degree to which Ozu's film is indebted to McCarey's. But as this essay has shown, the number and nature of the similarities are undeniable and strikingly persuasive. In short, as David Bordwell has said, in *Tokyo Story* Ozu "recasts" *Make Way for Tomorrow*.

NOTES

1. See, e.g., Keiko I. McDonald, "A Basic Narrative Mode in Yasujirō Ozu's *Tokyo Story*," in her *Cinema East: A Critical Study of Major Japanese Films* (East Brunswick, NJ: Associated University Presses, 1983), 203; Tony Rayns, "*Tokyo Monogatari (Tokyo Story)*," *Sight and Sound*

4:2 (February 1994): 63 (reprinted in this volume); Charles Silver, "Leo McCarey: From Marx to McCarthy," *Film Comment* 9:5 (September–October 1973): 10. Silver has this to say about *Make Way for Tomorrow:* "It seems to me superior to that other brilliant treatment of the generation gap, Ozu's *Tokyo Story.*"

2. David Bordwell, *Ozu and the Poetics of Cinema* (Princeton, NJ: Princeton University Press, 1988), 328–9.

3. The *shomin-geki* was a broad-ranging genre that included such subgenres as the *sarariman* (salaryman) film, which dealt with white-collar workers and bureaucrats, the nonsense comedy, the *haha-mono* (mother film), and the home drama (with which in time it became virtually synonymous). As Audie Bock points out, the genre "may have somewhat overplayed hardship, but at least it did not gloss over life's real difficulties" (*Japanese Film Directors* [Tokyo: Kodansha, 1978], 75). Emphasizing character and social interaction more than plot, it proved to be a durable and distinguished genre that could accommodate various subjects, themes, and directorial styles. In the hands of Ozu, Shimazu Yasujiro, Gosho Heinosuke, Naruse Mikio, Kinoshita Keisuke, among others, it thrived from the mid-1920s well into the 1960s. After that, movie tastes changed, leaving the genre mainly to television and to nostalgic treatment (e.g., the "Tora-san" series of Yamada Yoji). For an overview of the *shomin-geki,* see Max Tessier, "Au film des saisons: Le cinéma 'intimiste' et 'familial,' " *Images du cinéma japonais* (Paris: Henri Veyrier, 1981), 47–67; and Joseph L. Anderson and Donald Richie, *The Japanese Film: Art and Industry,* expanded ed. (Princeton, NJ: Princeton University Press, 1982), 51–2, 96–102, 357–9, 362–3.

4. See Bordwell, *Ozu and the Poetics of Cinema,* 328–9, and Rayns, *"Tokyo Monogatari,"* 63.

5. See Tadao Sato, *Currents in Japanese Cinema,* trans. Gregory Barrett (Tokyo: Kodansha, 1982), 33–7, 185–6; Bordwell, *Ozu and the Poetics of Cinema,* 19–21.

6. Bordwell, *Ozu and the Poetics of Cinema,* 24.

7. According to Donald Richie, "In this picture Japanese critics see Ozu creating his first shomin-geki" (*Ozu* [Berkeley: University of California Press, 1974], 207). But apparently there is some difference of opinion. As Bordwell notes, Tadao Sato considers *Nikutaibi* (*Body Beautiful,* 1928) to be Ozu's first work in the genre (*Ozu and the Poetics of Cinema,* 186).

8. James Harvey, *Romantic Comedy in Hollywood: From Lubitsch to Sturges* (New York: Knopf, 1987), 268.

9. Kristin Thompson and David Bordwell, *Film History: An Introduction* (New York: McGraw-Hill, 1994), 235.

10. T. Harry Williams, Richard N. Current, and Frank Freidel, "The New Deal: Struggle for Reform," in *A History of the United States Since 1865* (New York: Knopf, 1959), 504–5.

11. For discussions of Japanese society see Chie Nakane, *Japanese Society* (Berkeley: University of California Press, 1970), and Chiye Sano, *Changing Values of the Japanese Family* (Washington, DC: Catholic University Press of America, 1958).

12. Yoshinori Kamo, "A Note on the Elderly Living Arrangements in Japan and the United States," in *Growing Old in America*, 4th ed., ed. Beth B. Hess and Elizabeth W. Markson (New Brunswick, NJ: Transaction, 1991), 460.

13. Quoted in Silver, "Leo McCarey," 10.

14. Ibid. Can there be said to be such a genre as "American *shomin-geki*"? Richie writes, "Ozu's films are a kind of home drama, a genre that in the West rarely attains the standard of art and that even now is generally perceived as second-rate" (*Ozu*, 1). Here we have an acknowledgment that such a genre (or a comparable genre) exists in the West. But obviously, it is more "melodramatic" than the Japanese genre, lacks that genre's realist bias, and is much less committed to depicting ordinariness. Still, there are films that seem equivalent, to various degrees, to those in the Japanese *shomin-geki*. *Make Way for Tomorrow* is certainly one such film. Others might include the Bluebird movies of the 1910s and 1920s; the films of Chaplin; some films from the 1920s and 1930s in the rural romance tradition (e.g., Griffith's *True Heart Susie* [1919], Vidor's *The Crowd* [1928] and *Our Daily Bread* [1934]; and in the 1940s, perhaps some of the "home front" dramas and social problem films; in the 1950s, the "slice-of-life" dramas about common people, like Mann's *Marty* (1955) and *The Bachelor Party* (1956) and Brooks and Chayefsky's *The Catered Affair* (1956), all heavily influenced by Italian neorealism.

Significantly, Japanese audiences were quick to see similarities between the *shomin-geki* and *Marty*. In fact, Anderson and Richie report that the American film "utterly failed . . . one criticism often heard was that it was 'too much like a Japanese film' " (*The Japanese Film*, 419). It is also quite possible that the genre occasionally "overlaps" other genres, e.g., romantic comedy. Since the 1960s, the "American *shomin-geki*" seems to have taken the same path as its Japanese counterpart, finding continued life (as "soap opera") on television. This subject merits further study.

15. Roger Dooley, *From Scarface to Scarlett: American Films in the 1930s* (San Diego and New York: Harvest / Harcourt Brace Jovanovich, 1979), 543.
16. McDonald, "A Basic Narrative Mode," 206.
17. Rayns, *"Tokyo Monogatari,"* 63.
18. See Bordwell, *Ozu and the Poetics of Cinema,* 224–9.
19. Ibid., 330.
20. McDonald, "A Basic Narrative Mode," 213.
21. Consult the Select Bibliography for a number of the most useful English-language studies of Ozu's cinema.
22. Robin Wood, "Leo McCarey," in *The International Dictionary of Films and Filmmakers.* Volume 2: *Directors and Filmmakers,* ed. Christopher Lyon (Chicago: St. James Press, 1984), 358; Silver, "Leo McCarey," 10.
23. Jonathan Rosenbaum, "Journals: Paris," *Film Comment* 9:6 (November–December 1973): 4.
24. Charles Affron, *Cinema and Sentiment* (Chicago: University of Chicago Press, 1982), 65.
25. Ibid.
26. Jeffrey Richards, "Great Moments: Leo McCarey," *Focus on Film,* no. 14 (Spring 1973): 37.
27. Harvey, *Romantic Comedy in Hollywood,* 255.
28. Ibid.
29. Jean-Pierre Coursodon with Pierre Sauvage, "Leo McCarey," *American Directors* (New York: McGraw-Hill, 1983), 1:252.
30. Wood, "Leo McCarey," 359.
31. Ibid.
32. McDonald, "A Basic Narrative Mode," 223–4; Raymond Carney, *"Tokyo Story (Tokyo Monogatari),"* in *Magill's Survey of Cinema: Foreign Language Films,* ed. Frank N. Magill (Englewood, NJ: Salem Press, 1985), 7:3121–2.
33. McDonald, "A Basic Narrative Mode," 224.
34. Paul Schrader, *Transcendental Style in Film: Ozu, Bresson, Dreyer* (New York: Da Capo Press, 1972), 48.
35. Richie, *Ozu,* 25–7.

2   Travel Toward and Away

FURUSATO AND JOURNEY IN *TOKYO STORY*

At sunset
on Asaji's moors
a traveller:
oh! where
will he find lodgings?

    (Minamoto no Tsunenobu,
    1016–97)[1]

The traveler dreams of destinations, of familiar faces, of sites whose names have been sung by poets, painters, and other travelers of the past. The suitcases are packed with necessities and with one or two objects that will lead the traveler's thoughts back to home. Loved ones, like the youngest daughter, Kyoko, in *Tokyo monogatari* (*Tokyo Story*, 1953) by Ozu Yasujiro, might go to see the traveler off at the station.

As we all know, however, the destination is not always as imagined. Once-familiar faces have aged, perhaps growing into more rigid masks with the years. Children seen years ago might be transformed completely. The splendors of one's destination might be as tarnished as an old brass pot too long in need of cleaning.

53

Then again, there is another possibility: someone at the end of the journey who had seemed a relative stranger could be discovered to be warm and caring, like Noriko, the young war widow of one of the sons of the Hirayama family. A city or house considered merely a point of passing could turn out to hold unexpected charms. The journey traveled is never the journey dreamed. The journey has its own logic and its own necessities. As several of the characters in *Tokyo Story* learn, the traveler who does not bend to this logic is broken by it.

Tokyo Story has often been regarded as one of the truest depictions of a specific historical moment, in this case the postwar period in Japan. On another level, it could also be considered "a picture so Japanese and at the same time so personal, and hence so universal in its appeal, that it becomes a masterpiece."[2] The repetition of patterns, the distinctive camera style, and the sense of stillness in Ozu's films have often been noted. What is less frequently commented upon is the powerful pull of movement in his films – movement that is both internal and external, leading toward and away.

The "hourglass structure" and the implied contrasts among characters are well-known elements of *Tokyo Story*, but there is an equally strong sense of continuity and cyclical motion at work in the film.[3] Donald Richie writes of Ozu's care in accurately presenting chronological travel, synchronizing the dialogue with the landscape through which the characters are traveling.[4] The stops on the journey include Tokyo, Atami, Osaka, Onomichi, and Tokyo again, but these specific geographical locations could be seen as only the skeletal structure of a far more important journey.

Images of trains open and close *Tokyo Story*. At first rooftops obscure the image of a train passing in the distance, but then the director "flips" this image and places the train directly and inescapably in the foreground of the shot. At the beginning of *Tokyo Story*, we are introduced to the world of the parents, Shukichi and his wife, Tomi, through a series of interior shots. Like the neighbor who stops by to inquire about their plans, we peer into the interior life of this elderly couple and try to piece together the fabric of their intended journey.

TRAVEL IN JAPAN: EXAMPLES FROM OTHER ART FORMS

What traditions does Ozu draw on in presenting his elderly travelers' visit to grown children who have moved away? To answer this question, let us make a digression through other images of the traveler in Japanese art forms predating the arrival of the cinema.

In the United States, travel tends to be associated with the "new frontier" and with a sense of hope, while in Japan the association tends to be that of separation from the group. For example, note this poignant statement of the Japanese poet Matsuo Basho (1644–94) before setting forth on one of his travels:

> The thought of the 3,000 *ri* ahead of us on the journey filled my heart with apprehension, and I shed tears of farewell at the crossroads of this realm of unreality. (*Narrow Roads to the Far North* [*Oku no hosomichi,* 1702])[5]

In Japanese travel literature (*kiko*), there is a general mystique to the image of a person embarking on a journey, be it the tale of one on a pleasure journey, a religious pilgrimage, or a journey in search of artistic inspiration. (Writings based on travels undertaken to make a living are not as common.) Traditionally there have been many reasons for travel in Japan: to see cherry blossoms in bloom, to enjoy maple leaves in autumn, to see Mt. Fuji or other historical and holy places. During the medieval period, travel was frequent partially because the government of the *shogun* in Edo was far from the site of the emperor's court in Kyoto. People would travel to place petitions, to visit relatives, or just out of curiosity, keeping travel diaries and stopping at inns along the way. The ideal of the Heian courtier was carried over in travel writing, even into more militaristic and troubled times.

A comic depiction of a journey was recorded in Jippensha

Ikku's *Shanks' Mare* (*Tokaidochu Hizakurige*, 1802–9) about the exploits of two carefree travelers along the Tokaido highway.[6] Written in a colloquial, often vulgar language full of jokes and puns, the exploits of Kitahachi and Yajirobei (Kita and Yaji) won such widespread public accolades that the end of their Tokaido adventures in 1809 was greeted with cries for more (as were Tora-san's filmic adventures years later). So Ikku took his readers on a journey to the Buddhist shrine of Kompira on Shikoku in 1810, to Miyajima in 1811, and along the Kisokaido road from Gifu prefecture north to Nagano between 1812 and 1822. The writings about these two hapless heroes enjoyed a long lifetime, eventually stretching from 1802 to 1831. In his "introductory" writings (finally composed in 1814!), Ikku commented that in his stories "everything is mixed together as the goods in the shop of a general dealer."[7]

The two heroes meet other travelers on the road who know their part of Edo (but who also make up stories based more on nostalgia than on fact). Despite this nostalgia, they long for the road. In the opening of Book One, the heroes proclaim:

> Now is the time to visit all the celebrated places in the country and fill our heads with what we have seen, so that when we become old and bald we shall have something to talk about over the teacups.[8]

Along the road Kita and Yaji meet up with thieves, cunning priests, failed businessmen-turned-pilgrims. Trying to sneak into the beds of young female travelers, they invariably end up in some old woman's bed by mistake. Nevertheless, they try to reassure themselves that the bad times aren't really so bad. As the ending verse of the Tokaido writings proclaims: "Whether we start or whether we stay / The day we start is the luckiest day."

VISUAL ARTS

The Tokaido (literally "eastern sea route"), the road between Kyoto and Edo, traversed provinces controlled by *dai-*

myo (feudal lords). Barrier posts set up along the way divided the journey temporally and spatially. The great artist Hiroshige (1797–1858) sketched landscape scenes, fellow travelers, buildings, the "fifty-three stations" of the Tokaido.[9] In Hiroshige's time, a traveler could journey by horseback, on foot, or in *kago* (palanquin), stopping at inns along the way (Figure 18). Although literati artists rarely undertook such sketching journeys, some *nanga*-style artists like Tani Buncho (1763–1840) traveled along the Tokaido in 1793.[10]

Meisho-e (pictures of famous places) often depicted places that had been immortalized in poetry; in fact, more often than not, the painters never left home but rather recorded their visual impressions after reading the poems. In the same way, poets writing of the hardships and rewards of travel may never have strayed from the comforts of their country villas.[11]

In the same vein, landscape painting in Chinese and Japanese art is often painting not from nature but rather from memory.[12] Concerns with verisimilitude take second place to expressions of feelings or a state of mind. The point of view is often not that of the individual, but that of an observer somehow suspended in space, transcending the immediate and momentary.

PERFORMERS

Wandering storytellers trace their roots back to Buddhist missionaries whose colorful narratives enlivened their preaching. These traveling priests often carried *oi* (cabinets, like a kind of backpack) full of sutras, altar objects, and a few personal objects.[13] Barbara Ruch points out that wandering priests and nuns (Kumano bikuni) often adapted vocal literature (which she calls *onsei bungaku*, or "audience-oriented repertory literature") to fit their missionary purposes.[14] These wandering storytellers, also known as *etoki hoshi* or simply as secular *etoki*, helped to popularize the *emakimono* (picture scroll) format. Religious instruction was probably not the sole purpose of these medieval travelers – raising funds for home temples or finding companions on the road may have been other motivations. A common

FIGURE 18

Hokusai (1760–1849), *Waterfall,* Japanese *ukiyo-e* school, color woodblock. (Courtesy of the Cleveland Museum of Art; gift of Mr. and Mrs. J. H. Wade [16.1137].)

belief in the magical power of their vocal presentations contributed to their general acceptance. Ruch notes other "wandering proselytizers and jongleurs" during this period, including the blind *biwa hoshi,* who helped formalize great works of epic literature, and the blind female *goze,* who recited narratives to the accompaniment of the *tsuzumi* drum.[15]

In the traditional theater, the travel motif is highlighted in the *michiyuki* of a priest in noh or of star-crossed lovers in kabuki. The *michiyuki* is a technique that depicts characters' movements, often by a series of symbolically significant place names. The *michiyuki* tradition is tied not only to the themes of traditional plays but also to the physical structure of the stage of the noh and kabuki theaters. Both theaters have passageways attached to the main stage at one end, reinforcing the sense of the actor or actors traveling from one point to another. In the noh theater, the *hashigakari* is positioned at a distance from the audience, but this allows the audience to view the actors from a profile angle as the actors slowly enter the performance area. This passageway is actually a bridge that joins the stage diagonally at upstage right. It relates to the moving between two worlds, the phenomenological and the supernatural. In fact, the original meaning of the word *hashigakari* is "suspension bridge."

Time and space in the noh theater are purely theatrical in that they change only within the mind of the audience. In the noh *michiyuki,* the secondary actor (*waki*), who is usually a priest, enters on the *hashigakari* on a pilgrimage. He announces his identity and then continues to "travel," stating the names of the places he is "passing." There is no scenery rolling by in the background; in fact, there is no scenery in noh drama at all. Without moving more than a few feet, the *waki* can travel a hundred miles. Through his recitation of the *michiyuki* near the beginning of the play, this *waki* character helps join the living with the spirits of the dead.

In an article entitled "Ritual Drama: Between Mysticism and Magic," David George proposes that the audience in the noh theater also joins in the *michiyuki.*[16] George sees the audience, like the priest, embarking on a journey from the natural to the aesthetic. It is a journey that involves transformation, like the transformation of the main actor (*shite*) when his or her true identity is revealed. The noh *michiyuki* can thus be compared to a kind of shamanistic act.

In the kabuki theater, which postdates the noh theater, the *hanamichi* passageway provides an intimate acting area passing directly through the audience. Kabuki scholar Earle Earnst has pointed out that when an actor enters on the *hanamichi*, the audience turns physically toward that extension of the stage, as one does when an important person enters the room.[17] Like the *hashigakari* of the noh theater, the kabuki *hanamichi* acts as a kind of "fade out" and "fade in" for characters, to use cinematic terms. Even after an actor has made a dramatic exit along these passageways, a sort of trailing note remains in the air, like the trailing notes (*yoin*) in a Japanese musical composition.

CINEMATIC ANTECEDENTS

In his study of archetypes in the Japanese cinema, Gregory Barrett divides what he calls the "wanderer archetype" into three categories: the exile, the pilgrim, and the vagabond.[18] The exile is marked by his (or, in rare cases, her) yearning for home, for an end to the loneliness of separation from the nurturing group. The exile image can be traced from Susano O to Prince Genji and up to contemporary *yakuza* (gangster) film characters.[19] The *matatabi mono,* a subgenre of the *jidaigeki* that deals with wandering outlaws and gamblers, shows travelers whose courage is often motivated by a profound sense of despair arising from a feeling of exclusion from the group. The *toseinin* character (literally "a person who wanders through the world") does not really belong to any group, although he tends to find lodging at the house of a *yakuza* gang and sometimes fights to help the gang members out. His basic nature, however, is that of one who is always on the move.

The pilgrim, in Barrett's view, sees this world as only a tempo-

FIGURE 19
The vagabond figure: Tora-san.

rary dwelling, and he or she travels in search of religious truths. The rigors of travel become a means of penance or of thanksgiving. In contrast, a vagabond (like the Tora-san character in the *It's Hard to Be a Man* [*Otoko wa tsurai yo*] series by Yamada Yoji) is a happy-go-lucky wanderer who prefers the carefree life with all its hardships to the restrictions of life in society (Figure 19). Barrett considers this archetype of the vagabond a problematic one that does not fit neatly into the conservative schemata or the (later) antitheses of those conservative archetypes that he outlines.[20] Rather, the wanderer at times is in concordance with traditional roles, at other times transcends or is even opposed to them.

The mixture of pathos and comedy in cinematic wanderers, like the characters in Ozu Yasujiro's Kihachimono films (e.g., *A Story of Floating Weeds* [*Ukigusa monogatari*, 1934, remade as *Ukigusa* in 1959]), contrasts with the image of the tormented traveler, or the traveler in pursuit of self-knowledge, seen in films like Mizoguchi Kenji's *White Threads of the Cascades* (*Taki no shiraito*, 1933) and *The Life of Oharu* (*Saikaku ichidai onna*, 1952), Shindo Kaneto's *The Solitary Travels of Chikuzan, Tsugaru Shamisen Player* (*Chikuzan hitori tabi*, 1978), or Shinoda Masahiro's *Banished Orin* (aka *Melody in Gray, Hanare goze Orin*, 1977) about a blind *shamisen* player.[21] As Barrett points out, these latter characters come closer to the archetype of pilgrim than to the role of vagabond.

In his film *The Straits of Love and Hate* (*Aienkyo*, 1937), Mizoguchi shows how the protagonist Ofumi comes to realize that an insecure life among traveling artists is to be preferred to security among those who persist in treating her like a servant. As in the earlier *White Threads of the Cascade*, however, the life of the traveling performer is not romanticized. Marching with instruments through lonely villages, performing in small rural theaters to nearly empty halls, trying to calm a feverish baby on crowded trains – all of these travails are suggested both visually and through dialogue. In *Story of the Last Chrysanthemum* (*Zangiku monogatari*, 1939), the director even shows the traveling performers being displaced from their hall by a group of hefty female wrestlers. Mizoguchi was the kind of director who would always side with those who were most fragile and would take great care to reveal such characters' inner strengths and resilience.

Journeys also play a decisive role in films like *The Ballad of Narayama* (*Narayama bushi-ko*, 1958 [by Kinoshita Keisuke] and

1983 [by Imamura Shohei]), Kurosawa's *The Men Who Tread on the Tiger's Tail* (*Tora no O o fumu otokotachi,* 1945), and Mizoguchi's *Ugetsu* (*Ugetsu monogatari,* 1953). Films based on theatrical sources in which lovers must travel to find a space in which they can express their love – a journey that often leads to death – include Shinoda Masahiro's *Double Suicide* (*Shinju ten no amijima,* 1969) and Mizoguchi's *A Story of Chikamatsu* (*Chikamatsu monogatari,* 1954).

A quite different view of the traveler is found in the image of the naive and enthusiastic Japanese tourist that continues to inspire filmmakers. Japanese characters in American film director Jim Jarmusch's film *Mystery Train* (1989), set in Memphis, Tennessee, present another interpretation of the life of the Japanese traveler. The viewer observes the traveler through an ingenious triptych format. The first sequence, entitled "Far from Yokohama," is an Admiral Perry story in reverse. Two Japanese tourists, a young man, Jun (Nagase Masatoshi), and his girlfriend, Mitsuko (Kudo Yuki), arrive in Memphis, the home of their heroes, Elvis Presley and Carl Perkins, to breathe in – for a day or two – the "grandeur" of their imagined rock-and-roll haven. With his slicked-back hair and her fluorescent pink lipstick, they have adopted the trademarks of the form without its essence. "If sixty percent of the buildings were taken away, this would look just like Yokohama," Jun proclaims, effectively placing himself in an imaginary landscape.

Unable to fathom the thick and fast southern English, they remain in the Memphis of their fantasy. Unlike Luisa (Nicoletta Braschi), the somewhat more savvy Italian woman in the second part of this film, entitled "A Ghost," the Japanese remain within their learned behavior – the cigarette pulled from behind the ear, the lighter deftly flipped open – as if on a movie set.

Yet this satiric, but gentle look at obsessed foreigners and the equally odd assortment of Americans "lost in space" (the title of the third part) also shows the connections. Musical motifs like Elvis's "Blue Moon," a shared disappointment that there is no television set in the seedy hotel room, even a mysterious gunshot tie together not only the filmic structure but also the strangers in this strange world. Somehow the connections in films like these make the foreignness less foreign, and the passing of different lives seem closer, than we had imagined.

FILMMAKING AS JOURNEY

Ozu made *Tokyo Story* when he was fifty years old, and his career is itself a kind of journey – one marked by a strong commitment to his own time frame and urgencies. His career spanned thirty years, from his beginning as an assistant cameraman with Shochiku in 1923, his start as an assistant director in 1926, and his entry into directorial ranks one year later. His early training with one of Shochiku's lesser directorial talents, Okubo Tadamoto (who specialized in *"nansensu"* [i.e., nonsense] comedies), helped reinforce Ozu's natural gift for comedy. Although his later films often focus on serious themes presented in a stately, subdued manner, Ozu always recalled that life requires its moments of comedy. As David Owens notes, "Ozu had an earthy sense of humor attuned to the silly rituals and fantasies of little boys and old men, between which he found strong parallels."[22]

Resisting the "talkie" movement until 1936 (with *The Only Son* [*Hitori musuko*]) and color films until 1958 (with *Equinox Flower* [*Higanbana*]), Ozu set his own pace and did not rush into new possibilities. With the stoicism and resolve frequently seen in the older characters in his films, Ozu accepted new technologies only when doing otherwise became impossible. Relying on the elegance of the simple cut, Ozu concentrated on the precision of actions beneath which feelings are hidden.

As an assistant director to Ozu in 1957, Shinoda Masahiro called him "Professor Keyhole," describing the lens of his camera as "a keyhole in the door of Death."[23] Commenting on the way actor Ryu Chishu never seemed to move in a particular scene, Shinoda stated:

But from my vantage point behind Ozu's massive shoulder, I saw Ozu gazing through his lens at Ryū's erect back as if Ryū were continually fading away down a distant road.[24]

As Shinoda noted, Ozu's stationary camera could give a profound sense of life's movement. Sato Tadao has commented that, in Ozu's films, the audience is rarely shown lateral movements or partial views of a character; rather, backward and forward movements and full-face shots are preferred.[25] Just as the camera focuses only on what is directly in front of the lens, so do we, as viewers of an Ozu film, focus only on what is directly before us, unadorned, unembellished.

In his *Transcendental Style in Film: Ozu, Bresson, Dreyer*, Paul Schrader poetically states that "like the traditional Zen artist, Ozu directs silences and voids."[26] To this one could add that Ozu creates a world in which he can live – a world that holds meaning for him, that creates a family for him. The patterns that Ozu establishes within his films, and among individual films, point not only to the patterns that define our lives but also to what lies outside those patterns.

The use of the journey motif in Ozu's oeuvre did not begin with *Tokyo Story*. Trains open and close other Ozu films, like *Equinox Flower*.[27] Commenting on the "humanized, or anthropomorphized" nature of trains in Japanese films (in contrast to their use as a symbol of the power of the modern age in the West), Donald Richie notes:

> Although much influenced by the modernist-accented American cinema, Ozu found no intrinsic value in pounding pistons and hurtling cowcatchers. Rather, he saw in the train a device that could reinforce and make visible the various structures of the film.[28]

Ozu even goes so far as to make one of the Hirayama children, Keizo, an employee of the railroad to further humanize the image of the train. Nevertheless, he reminds us that it was trains that took Keizo away on business so he missed being with his mother before she died. The brightness and openness of the first shots in Onomichi, with its peaceful harbor and gently sloping rooftops, are contrasted with the shots of the crowded train station when the parents leave Tokyo. Figures rushing toward the train block our view.

David Bordwell points out that Ozu offers a "highly unified plot construction" and presents symmetries, parallels, cycles, repeated motifs, and repeated general plot components in his films.[29] At times Ozu plays with these patterns, even misleading the viewer, who anticipates a particular connection. However, as Bordwell notes, "when a single event finds a spot within all these structures, it gains an enormous narrative richness."[30] Such an event and pattern in an Ozu film often constitute a journey.

Travels to Tokyo are common in Ozu's films: in *I Graduated, But . . .* (*Daigaku wa deta keredo,* 1929) and *College Is a Nice Place* (*Daigaku yoi toko,* 1936), the college graduate comes to Tokyo to look for employment. In *The Only Son,* the mother comes to Tokyo to visit her son and experiences a different kind of reception there. *Passing Fancy* (*Dekigokoro,* 1933) shows the father going off to start a new job, leaving the son behind (but returning before he is halfway to the new city). As Donald Richie points out, this pattern is seen in reverse in films like *Late Autumn* (*Akibiyori,* 1960) and *An Autumn Afternoon* (*Samma no aji,* 1962). In *Late Spring* (*Banshun,* 1949), the father and daughter take a last trip, to Kyoto, before the father gives her away in marriage.

Most of Ozu's earlier films are set in the *shitamachi* (downtown, working-class) area of Tokyo.[31] With *What Did the Lady Forget?* (*Shukujo wa nani o wasureta ka,* 1937), Ozu moved the setting of his films to a modern "uptown" section. In *Tokyo Story,* Noriko takes her former in-laws on a bus tour of Tokyo. Despite the tour guide's attempts to "trace the history of a great city," the elderly couple can understand Tokyo only as the locale of a handful of people they know. Gazing out at the vast expanse of tall, concrete buildings, so much in contrast to the gentle rooflines and seascape of Onomichi, the mother asks the father,

"What part of Tokyo are we in?" and he can only reply vaguely, "A suburb."

Earlier, the mother had commented to Noriko that Tokyo seemed so far away, but now she sees that it can be reached in a day by train. One cannot help but wonder, however, if this is really the city of Tokyo she has reached or some internal destination. In a reversal of roles, the young widow becomes the maternal one – offering shelter, the couple's favorite foods, even a small allowance (*okozukai*). Noriko's polite solicitousness contrasts with the tendency of the Hirayama children to talk about their parents as if they were children who could be easily amused by some cheap trifle. The elderly parents seem to be constantly packing and unpacking their bags, not only because they are being shuttled from one child's place to another but also, it seems, because these objects are their links to a gentler time.

In an article entitled "Attitudes Toward Tokyo on Film," Richie notes that – in contrast to the Western tendency to show the modern city as a place of promise – early Japanese films tended to stress a nostalgia for *furusato* (hometown).[32] Later, in accordance with Western cinematic patterns, the depiction of city-as-evil developed in Japanese films. On the other hand, there has also been a move toward the "rehabilitating city-film genre" in which the evil city is shown to possess warmer, *furusato*-like qualities.[33] *Tokyo Story* partakes of all three themes: nostalgia for *furusato,* city-as-evil, and the appearance of *furusato*-like moments even in the coldest city. In a drunken, remorseful mood in a bar with two old acquaintances, Shukichi complains that "there are too many people in Tokyo" – too much competition, too little opportunity. In this way, he searches for excuses for the callousness of his grown children.

Ozu also includes, or implies, journeys of a longer distance in his films. *Brothers and Sisters of the Toda Family* (*Toda-ke no kyodai,* 1941) ends with the planned move of the mother and youngest daughter to China. *Early Summer* (*Bakushu,* 1951) shows the daughter planning to marry and move to Akita in northern Japan, bringing on the dissolution of her family. The journey is

FIGURE 20
Traveling performers in *Floating Weeds* (*Ukigusa*, 1959).

integral to the reconciliation of the estranged couple in *Early Spring* (*Soshun*, 1956), as the husband accepts a transfer to a position in the countryside, where the wife joins him. *The Flavor of Green Tea over Rice* (*Ochazuke no aji,* 1952) even includes the announcement of a trip to Uruguay and a shot of an airplane taking off. *Floating Weeds* begins with an image of a boat – the arrival of a troupe of traveling performers – and ends with the sound and movement of a train. In the famous closing scene, Sumiko (Kyo Machiko) and Komajuro (Nakamura Ganjiro) meet at the train station and decide to forget their differences and continue on the journey together (Figure 20). Everything has changed; nothing has changed; everything has changed.

JOURNEY AND MEMORY

The journey outward is toward knowledge; the return, toward rest. Each journey depicted by Ozu is an inward journey,

FIGURE 21
Seeing and being seen: characters in Ozu's *The End of Summer*
(*Kohayakawake no aki*, 1961).

despite its stated goals. The father and mother in *Tokyo Story* are
not traveling to see their city-dwelling children as much as they
are hoping to confirm that their life's work has been worthwhile.
They journey in search of echoes, and they return from their
journey with the awareness that things could have been worse –
that to be greedy is to lose even what they have. The forgiveness
the mother shows toward her forgetful husband in the opening
dialogue about the "air pillow" (*kuki makura*) is later echoed in
the sense of acceptance Shukichi learns to feel toward his less
than perfect children.

Like the *waki* in the noh theater, travel for Ozu is initiation
into change. The people in his film do not travel to see but to be
seen, eternally watched by forces greater than themselves (Figure
21). The more mundane the situation, the more profound its
implications – what other director has captured this realization
with such gentle acerbity, such refinement?

FIGURE 22
Emptiness and fullness: from the Atami resort sequence in *Tokyo Story*.

The day is bright . . . children in uniform hurry to school . . . a woman folds the laundry . . . a grandmother takes her small grandson to play on a hillside . . . and suddenly life changes irrevocably. No one knew the power of the everyday like Ozu, and no one presented it with less ornamentation.

The elderly couple stare out at the water surrounding the seaside resort of Atami. The mother feels faint for a moment. Ozu shows how small the two appear against the natural and commercial, manmade forces that surround them. At first he records the scene with a long shot but quickly moves in to focus on the two figures, reminding us that these two small human forms are what give weight to the image. Yet, like the seemingly solitary shots of vases, hillsides, and laundry hung out to dry, the human figures in Ozu's films are both essential and transitory, eventually passing from the frame. Empty rooms are not really empty – they are full of the presence of people who were there before, and of the memory of people (Figure 22). Ozu holds the shot just a few seconds longer than we might expect in order to remind us of this.

Noriko returns from her extended stay in Onomichi, glancing at the watch her father-in-law has given her. But this is a film not about time, but rather about movement through time. Noriko faces forward. As she admitted to her former father-in-law after the funeral: "There are days when I don't even remember your son . . . days that seem to be full of waiting." The father will probably never return to Tokyo, and Noriko's visits to Onomichi will become less frequent, if they happen at all. Will Noriko heed the urging of Shukichi and Tomi that she remarry and move beyond the past? In contrast to the relatively closed paths of the two oldest children, Koichi and Shige, and the journey of the youngest Kyoko (which has hardly begun), Noriko's journey is now an open one. She points out to Kyoko that children begin to drift away from their parents with time. It is fitting that the father and Noriko are the two main characters we see at the end of the film. The continuation of the story remains in their hands.

Left alone by his wife's death, the father realizes that he wishes he had been kinder to her while she was still living. This same realization comes to the youngest son. Father and son both return with the awareness of misdirections.

Ozu's films appear to move slowly, even at times to meander, but the rigorous geometry of his vision sets up a frame so inexorable that one finds essential images in it again and again. And there, just behind Hara Setsuko's resigned smile and the wintry form of the widowed father, lies a chasm so unavoidable that all the traveling toward and away becomes nothing but the movement of creatures trying to build a shelter in the face of possible storms and human destruction. But what magnificent structures are lined up so precisely on the tatami mats in the Hirayama home! Ozu points first to the "simple" surface, then to the chasm, then back to the wonder of that same surface.

Bordwell refers to *Tokyo Story* as didactic, and Ozu himself referred to it as his most melodramatic film.[34] This might be so, but *Tokyo Story* also fits the description of a superlative film offered by Russian film director Andrei Tarkovsky in his *Sculpting in Time:*

> Just as life, constantly moving and changing, allows everyone to interpret and feel each separate moment in his own way, so too a real picture, faithfully recording on film the time which flows on beyond the edges of the frame, lives within time if time lives within it; this two-way process is a determining factor of cinema.[35]

Trains carry passengers toward and away. Where are they going, these travelers? What have they found at the end of their journeys? When do their journeys end? *Tokyo Story* ends with the sounds of a clock ticking and a boat passing out to sea.

Travel is made up of arrivals and destinations; one never remains in either state for long. Ozu reminds us of this in the silly English lesson recited woodenly by Minoru, the oldest grandson: "The cold winter is over. Spring has come. It is April now."

The destination of the journey is inside each character. When the film is over, we realize that the destination of the journey is inside each of us as well.

NOTES

1. A poem written for the theme "Seeing a Traveller at Twilight": "Yuhi sasu / Asajigahara no / tabibito wa / aware izuku ni / yado o karuran."

     The term *furusato* in Japanese can be defined as "hometown," which is often viewed in an idealized light.
2. Donald Richie, *Ozu* (Berkeley: University of California Press, 1974), 239.
3. Note Donald Richie's discussion of the "hourglass format" of the film (Hawaii International Film Festival film showing, 1987) and Keiko I. McDonald, *Cinema East: A Critical Study of Major Japanese Films* (Rutherford, NJ: Fairleigh Dickinson University Press, 1983), 218: "Ozu's magnificent juxtaposition of the static and the mobile."
4. Richie, *Ozu,* 163–8.

5. Cited in Donald Keene, *Travelers of a Hundred Ages* (New York: Holt, 1989), 184. A *ri* can be considered an indication of immeasurable distance.

6. Ikku Jippensha (1765–1831) was the pen name of Shigeta Sadakazu.

7. Ikku Jippensha, *Shanks' Mare*, trans. Thomas Satchell (Rutland, VT: Tuttle, 1972), 19.

8. Ibid., 23. Several Japanese films, notably before the 1960s, center around the exploits of Kita and Yaji – for example, Chiba Yasuki's *Travel Chronicles of Yaji and Kita* (*Yaji-Kita dochuki*, 1958).

9. Hiroshige was only one of many Edo-period artists who produced picture books and individual prints of the Tokaido road between Edo (present-day Tokyo) and Osaka. Other artists of note include Rito Akizato, Ekken Kaibara, and Moronobu Hishikawa. For further details, see Narazaki Muneshige, *Hiroshige: The 53 Stations of the Tokaido* (Tokyo: Kodansha, 1974), 18–25.

10. The *nanga* school landscapes from the seventeenth century displayed a new sense of intimacy and immediacy, with figures based on Chinese models from the Ming dynasty. These *nanga* school painters tended to paint famous locales, adding their own touches.

11. The first eight imperial poetry anthologies included many travel poems: the *Kokinshu* (sixteen travel poems, forty-one parting poems), the *Gosenshu* (eighteen travel poems, forty-six parting poems), the *Shuishu* (no travel poems, thirty-three parting poems), the *Goshuishu* (thirty-six travel poems, thirty-nine parting poems), the *Kin'yoshu* (no travel poems, sixteen parting poems), the *Shinkashu* (no travel poems, fifteen parting poems), the *Senzaishu* (forty-seven travel poems, twenty-two parting poems), and the *Shinkokinshu* (ninety-four travel poems, thirty-nine parting poems). (These figures were given by Ivo Smits, Leiden University, in his presentation, "Imagined Hardships: Travel Poetry in Late Heian Japan," at the European Association of Japanese Studies conference, Copenhagen, 1994.)

12. Chinese monochrome landscape painting was brought to Japan by Ch'an Buddhist monks during the thirteenth century, and Japanese *shigajiku* (landscape and poem paintings) and *sansuiga* (landscape paintings) developed according to Chinese norms (1333–1573). This style of landscape painting developed during the Muromachi period, as Japan embarked on large-scale trading missions to China and as monks traveled back and forth between the two countries. Painters of the Kano and Unkoku schools and followers of Hasegawa Tohaku were particularly adept at Ch'an-style landscapes.

13. Note Kato Hidetoshi, "Japanese Popular Culture Reconsidered," in

Handbook of Japanese Popular Culture (New York: Greenwood Press, 1989), 305.

14. Barbara Ruch, "Medieval Jongleurs and the Making of a National Literature," in *Japan in the Muromachi Age,* ed. John Whitney Hall and Toyoda Takeshi (Berkeley: University of California Press, 1977), 285–91, 299.

15. Ibid., 307.

16. David George, "Ritual Drama: Between Mysticism and Magic," *Asian Theatre Journal* 4:2 (Spring 1987): 127–65.

17. Earle Earnst, *The Kabuki Theatre* (Honolulu: University Press of Hawaii, 1974), 97.

18. Gregory Barrett, *Archetypes in Japanese Film: The Sociopolitical and Religious Significance of the Principal Heroes and Heroines* (Selinsgrove, PA: Susquehanna University Press, 1989), 77–98.

19. Susano O is a Shinto god who was exiled from the Plain of Heaven because of his misbehavior. Prince Genji, the central character in *The Tale of Genji (Genji monogatari,* A.D. 1000), was exiled from the Heian-period court because of political intrigue.

20. The conservative archetypes listed by Barrett include "the Loyal Retainer and the Tormented Lord" and "the Vengeful Spirit," while the modern archetypal antitheses include "the Angry Young Man" and "the Earthy Woman."

21. Shindo's film is based on the true story of the blind shamisen performer Takahashi Chikuzan. Shinoda's film about the *goze* (blind shamisen players) is set in the early twentieth century.

22. David Owens, "Ozu Yasujiro," in *Kodansha Encyclopedia of Japan* 6 (1983), 142.

23. Leonard Schrader, *The Masters of Japanese Film* (unpublished manu- script), co-translated with Nakamura Haruji and Saito Chieko, 322– 3.

24. Sato Tadao, *Currents in Japanese Cinema,* trans. Gregory Barrett (Tokyo: Kodansha, 1982), 188.

25. Richie, *Ozu,* 153.

26. Paul Schrader, *Transcendental Style in Film: Ozu, Bresson, Dreyer* (Berkeley: University of California Press, 1972), 28.

27. See Hasumi Shigehiko, "Ozu Yasujirō to iu na no kisha wa kyō mo hashiritsuzukeru" (A train called Ozu Yasujirō continues to run today [interview with cinematographer Atsuta Yuharu]), *Lumière* 4 (1986): 17–24.

28. Donald Richie, "Trains in Japanese Film," in *Junction and Journey* (exhibition catalog), ed. Laurence Kardish (New York: Museum of Modern Art, June 21–October 1, 1991), 33.

29. David Bordwell, *Ozu and the Poetics of Cinema* (Princeton, NJ: Princeton University Press, 1988), 52–63.

30. Ibid., 61.

31. For a further description of the *shitamachi* atmosphere, see Edward Seidensticker, *Low City, High City: Tokyo from Edo to the Earthquake, 1867–1923* (New York: Knopf, 1983); its sequel, *Tokyo Rising: The City Since the Great Earthquake* (New York: Knopf 1990); and Theodore C. Bestor, "Conflict, Legitimacy, and Tradition in a Tokyo Neighborhood," in *Japanese Social Organization,* ed. Takie Sugiyama Lebra (Honolulu: University of Hawaii Press, 1992), 23–47.

32. Donald Richie, "Attitudes Toward Tokyo on Film," *East–West Film Journal* 3:1 (December 1988): 68–9.

33. Ibid., 72.

34. Bordwell, *Ozu and the Poetics of Cinema,* 329–30.

35. Andrei Tarkovsky, *Sculpting in Time: Reflections on the Cinema,* trans. Kitty Hunter-Blair (New York: Knopf, 1987), 118.

3 Ozu's Mother

Edo's culture was matriarchal, taking into its fold both good and bad sons. It was not a patriarchal culture that killed or drove away sons who weren't up to standard. It did not seek to attain purity through deductions and deletions. It continued to create something new through additions, mixture and blending. Now that the post–World War II period of singleminded modernization is over, the matriarchal, productive *katagi* [zeitgeist, character] of Edo and early Tokyo seems to be stirring again.

(Yuichiro Kojiro, "Edo: The City on the Plain")[1]

Tokyo Story is a quintessential city film, and cinema, as we know it, was born in the city. From the tiniest storefront peepshows to nickelodeon madness to the opulent picture palaces of the late 1920s, film exhibition was directed at concentrated masses of city dwellers clambering for admission to the latest attraction. Distributors devised the run-zone-clearance system to ensure thc fullest saturation of densely populated districts before turning to exploit more diffuse markets farther out. The diffusion of institutional cinema originally showed a centrifugal pattern outward from the metropolis (first from New York and Culver cities, before Hollywood occupied the center of the firmament) and, later, the post–World War I targeting of foreign countries to draw them into an orbit of dependency on American product. This outward diffusion of urban amusement took place at a time when rural and village life could be counted as an important touchstone, perhaps even a norm, for American cultural values.

Cinema as urban amusement phenomenon also carried changing renditions of city life in its imagery and narratives. City life was inscribed on film, not so much represented, in tandem with the outward diffusion of film amusement from its urban birthplace.[2] Cities provide standard props and backdrops for typical genres like detective thrillers and gangster stories, but in addition, specific cities themselves were personified – for example, in *Paris qui dort* (René Clair, 1924), *Tokyo Story* (Ozu Yasujiro, 1953), and *Manhattan* (Woody Allen, 1979). From the beginning, then, cities were employed generically and, in certain cases, as characters. *Man with a Movie Camera* (Dziga Vertov, 1929), *Berlin, Symphony of a City* (Walter Ruttmann, 1927), and *A propos de Nice* (Jean Vigo, 1930) all show nonfiction, experimental film leading the way in the personification of urban consciousness and its particular fittingness to yet another type of cinematic inscription.

The type of urban inscription on cinema that is the most fundamental and the most contemporary is the perceptual reorganization engendered by city life. Vertov's "Kino-eye" is the most literal visualization of this idea, revealing both its militancy and its liability. Vertov's direct, futurist identification of perception with machine was replaced by a more thoroughgoing, integrated urban inscription: the perceptual transformations undergone by characters and milieu initially outside the "cine-city" sphere of influence. The country naif confronting his nemesis in the overwhelming, voracious city is a virtual archetype of cinema (e.g., F. W. Murnau's 1927 *Sunrise*), following up on the pseudo-*actualité* of the bumpkin tearing down the movie screen to vanquish the villain (e.g., Edison's "Uncle Josh at the Moving Picture Show," 1902). This brings us back to the centrifugal pattern of film exhibition, transforming psychic as much as geographic frontiers, with its international counterpart of film export to countries subject to Euro-American influence and sometime hegemony.

What used to be known as the Third World has produced some of the most challenging work in cinematic reinscriptions of urban consciousness, from Satyajit Ray's Apu trilogy (1955–9) to *Manila in the Claws of Neon* (Lino Brocka, 1975) to the achievements of Taiwan New Cinema (Edward Yang, Hou Hsiao-hsien, et al.).[3] Ironically, it is the relative detachment and marginalization of these countries that occasion the most stark engagements with metropolitan presumptions and so reconfigure terms and conditions of the urban imaginary. The historical fact of uneven development brings basic issues of modernization and human rights, issues confronted by the West during the industrial revolution, into the global environment of the 1990s. Where, then, does Tokyo in the 1950s fit within these parameters? This is a complex question, but Ozu's *Tokyo Story* fundamentally engages the urban imaginary at a perceptual level, in addition to employing the other possible urban embodiments as genre and as city personification. Moreover, it is specifically Tokyo, rather than some generalized city, provoking a perceptual shift toward an urban imaginary that is maternal, though hardly nurturing in any traditional way.

Before considering Ozu, it is important to note that the artists just mentioned occupy different niches in their respective film industries; Ray's indifference to commercial Hindi cinema could not be more different from Brocka's passionate activism (and economic vulnerability) in the mainstream Manila film industry, including his reliance on stars and pulp genres. Hou Hsiao-hsien was a journeyman actor and assistant director in Taiwan, while

Edward Yang spent ten years in the United States before making his first film. Whatever else it is, Third World filmmaking is definitely not uniform. And while it is problematic to call Japan a Third World country, it is not going too far, I think, to characterize Tokyo in the early 1950s as "developing," and indeed well into the "singleminded modernization" mentioned by Kojiro in the epigraph.

Unlike the other directors just mentioned, Ozu enjoyed a position in Shochiku Studios that was not only secure, but central, and the consistency of his style and his quality gave him popularity as well as prestige. Ozu also considered himself a native Tokyoite ("Edokko," child of Edo), giving him an insider's vantage on the cinematic inscription of that city. The specific maternal associations of Ozu's native Tokyo, as well as Ozu's specific adjustments of Tokyo time-space, permit an accounting of the costs with which the city characters purchase their Tokyo affiliation. *Tokyo Story* shows an achievement of city identification through an exchange of older ties inherited from parents for affiliations of expediency and mutual interest. These new metropolitan affiliations are practical and probably necessary but (according to the viewpoint of real parents from the village) illusory. In the end, the story indeed belongs to Tokyo, but it is a Pyrrhic victory. We will see how this victory is achieved through the shuffling of kinship roles and the dilation of time in *Tokyo Story*. The concluding section discusses these technical tricks in light of Tokyo's – and Edo's – historical evolution, ending with an argument about Ozu's "filial" style.

DAUGHTER/MOTHER/WIDOW

In many of Ozu's films there is an exchange or reversal of roles, most often between generations of a family. This motivates characters to rise above individual inclinations and appreciate their roles from a familial perspective. It also furthers the idea that individuals are nodes, or kernels, in some larger organic kinship entity. In *Tokyo Story*, there is a certain commutability between the roles of daughter, mother, and widow because each character takes on aspects of each role, like a game of musical chairs. Noriko (Hara Setsuko), the widow, holds the key to this game because she, unlike the mother and the daughter, recognizes the pattern and her movement within it. Toward the end of the film, when the eldest daughter, Shige, is about to go and prepare to visit her critically ill mother in Onomichi, she does a double-take. She tells her brother Koichi to meet her at the usual place in Tokyo station, then briskly moves out the doorway and starts to go out. But then she stops and turns, as if to say, "Come to think of it . . ." and comes back to the same place where she was just now speaking to Koichi. She is about to call out to him, but abruptly she turns back, steps down into the *genkan* (entrance), and goes out the door. End of scene.

Why does she take her leave, then come back in, and finally turn around and complete her exit? What did the lady forget? When she first tries to leave, she wonders whether to bring black funeral clothes on the trip and adds, with a smile, "Let's just hope that we won't have to use them." With characteristic efficiency, Shige has ensured that all possibilities are covered. She has already established, with Koichi's sympathy, how busy she is and how troublesome this trip will be to her business as a hairdresser. Always looking ahead, she has foreseen the worst possible outcome and, visibly brightening, resolves not to be left unprepared. She has also uttered the obligatory expressions of worry over her mother's health.

But she has also remembered her mother's words at the station when seeing her parents off. Citing the great distance between Tokyo and Onomichi, her mother tells the Tokyo children not to worry if anything should happen to her. They needn't come all the way to Onomichi. In response, Shige had chided her: "Don't say such things; this isn't a final farewell!" With Kyoko's ominous telegram now in hand she has recalled, come to think of it, that it must have been a premonition. Perhaps the realization that this could actually happen, and may not be merely the superstition of an old country woman, is what gives

Shige pause; but before it enters her conscious mind she has bustled off to attend to practical matters.

In Onomichi, once the premonition has played out, Shige casually asks Kyoko for her mother's clothes and other keepsakes. She recalls, just as casually, the dizzy spell her mother had had while in Atami. But she never makes the incriminating connection between her preoccupation with her own business affairs and her scheme to send her parents off to Atami for a vacation – that is, to vacate them from her busy schedule. Shige's Tokyo priorities of getting ahead and avoiding waste do not allow her to entertain the possibility that her unfilial selfishness may have hastened her mother's illness and death. She is not deaf or insensitive to her mother's feelings; she is dimly aware of them, but she does not register them strongly enough. They simply cannot penetrate her callous urban shell. Shige's mother has not been completely banished from her daughter's thoughts, but "mother" is merely an echo, only rarely sounding notes of resemblance and recollection. Perhaps this echo is hinted at in Shige's uncharacteristic second-thought gesture.

The probable war widow Noriko, who seems the polar opposite of Shige's crass urbanity, takes over Shige's (and Koichi's) lapsed filial responsibility to her in-laws. Noriko looks after (*mendo miru*) the old couple in the way Shige and Koichi should, but do not. Noriko is a surrogate for the old couple's real children, just as the busy city lives of Shige and Koichi effectively substitute for their filial responsibilities. When Shige calls Noriko to ask her to take her parents out for the day, Shige clearly admits that she is passing the buck by repeating, "Warui wa ne . . ." ("It's awful of me, but . . ."). Noriko, for her part, does not mind in the least.

Noriko is urged both by Tomi and by Shukichi to forget her missing husband and remarry, but she remains oddly steadfast. Tomi is touched and slightly upset about her kindness to them. While Shukichi is out pickling himself with sake, Noriko lies supine next to Tomi, silently listening to her weeping over her fidelity to their missing son. The next morning she gives Tomi some money for the trip home. This shifting of emotional (and financial) burden onto Noriko puts her in a maternal position of endurance and fortitude, the proverbial "shoulder to cry on," but it also establishes her secret, which she confesses to Shukichi after Tomi's death.

Noriko's secret is this: she is not showing kindness to the old couple out of obligation to her late husband, but allows them to believe that she is. She insists that she is not a good woman, an honest woman, as Shukichi says, but is actually *zurui*. This is translated as "selfish" in the subtitles, but it really means crafty, cunning, or duplicitous. Noriko emerges as an urban chameleon, a type of trickster, though of a singularly benevolent kind. Although her in-laws are grateful to her because she continues to be filial eight years after her husband has disappeared (his body has never been found), in fact she is gratifying herself, not discharging filial obligations. She knows she is not bound by these obligations, but enjoys bringing happiness to the old folks, and she makes a conscious choice to treat them like the parents they once were. When Shige effectively vacates her position as a dutiful daughter, it becomes that much easier for Noriko to slip into the role she *chooses* to play. With the disappearance of her husband, Noriko's kinship with the family is suspended; therefore, the same kindness extended by an unrelated person that is obligatory for a family member is magnified and gains Noriko an extra measure of gratitude and regard. Perhaps this is the source of Noriko's confession of *zurui:* her superior knowledge of her (lack of) feeling toward her lost husband, combined with her awareness of the lack of warmth of her brothers- and sisters-in-law. This leads to a reputation for fidelity and filiality toward her in-laws that is actually misplaced (see diagram). Noriko thus reveals her own form of urban guile.

"A married daughter is a stranger," Shukichi remarks to Tomi about how Shige has changed. She has her own nuclear family, her hairdressing business, and her sharp Tokyo efficiency. Although he is not surprised, it is as if Shige has tricked her parents and become someone else. Here, too, the subtitles do not exactly

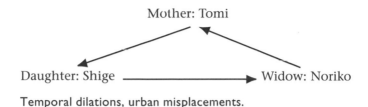

Temporal dilations, urban misplacements.

render his musing that when a daughter marries, "it is finished" (*oshimai ja*). He uses the same phrase, "Could this be the end?" when he is told that his wife Tomi is about to die (*Kore de oshimai kana?*). But while resting with Tomi in Osaka, he fails to understand the postwar metropolitan alchemy that somehow produces a daughter in Noriko from the loss of a son in the war. Their parental presence in Tokyo, while disillusioning, is what brings forth a daughter from Noriko's widowhood.

The commutability between the roles of mother, daughter, and widow is paralleled by the malleability of Tokyo time and space. Ozu "leapfrogs" and doubles back in the chronology of *Tokyo Story*. He also takes unexpected shortcuts in the space of Tokyo and Atami, revealing a playful, sometimes wicked sense of humor. Ozu's "trickster Tokyo" is an amplification of Noriko's *zurui* duplicitousness, a withholding of key links in a historical chain.[4]

The old folks spend just a week in Tokyo, including an overnight trip to Atami, a seaside playground popular with city folks. On the day of their return, Tomi and Shukichi are separated, and Ozu crosscuts between them. Here, the parallel between Tomi enjoying her evening with Noriko and Shukichi carousing with his old Onomichi mates is a crosscut sequence of simultaneity. A "meanwhile" separation of husband and wife shows what is happening at the same time in different places, suggesting parallels and contrasts between their separate experiences. Temporally and spatially, this sixth and final day in Tokyo forks in two, doubling its length for us as for its characters. The splitting of time here shows a dilation based on psychological investments, in turn depending on obstacles encountered by the old couple that lead to their separation.

Tokyo Day 6 begins early in Atami, where the scenery is good but where the old couple have had a very hard night. Shukichi observes, "This is a place for the younger generation," continuing a theme that will be magnified today, encompassing Tokyo and their own children. The trip to Atami was Shige's idea to get her parents out from underfoot in Tokyo, but in fact they inconvenience her further when they decide to return early. She is so peeved that she says they are "friends from the country" when someone from the shop asks who they are.[5] It is decided that Tomi will go stay with Noriko, and Shukichi with Hattori, from Onomichi. As they pack their things to prepare to leave Shige's, Shukichi wryly muses, "Well, we're homeless at last."

In a new location, a rare, exterior tracking shot shows the old couple resting on a curb at a temple and reflecting on "how vast Tokyo is" and "we would never meet again if we got lost." Here the two old people go their separate ways. In a subsequent scene Tomi recalls this was Ueno Park, the site of Kan'eiji, the family temple of the Tokugawa. The Tokugawa name is synonymous with the shogunate, its two-and-a-half-century feudal reign, and Edo (the pre-Meiji name for Tokyo), which owes its existence to the Tokugawa. Formerly "the abode of foxes," then coming to mark the graveyard of the Tokugawa hegemons, Ueno in the twentieth century served as habitat for the postwar homeless, particularly for migrant laborers from the North (and more recently from Iran) who arrived in Ueno station with no place to go.[6]

One thing that dilates psychological time even more than the old couple's separation is the respective themes of their conversations. The more Shukichi drinks with Numata and Hattori, the more bitter becomes their reminiscence. Shukichi demurs when his companion remarks on the lack of the old "fighting spirit," but once he hears that Numata lies about his son "the executive," he confesses that he too is disappointed with his children.

Meanwhile, Tomi recounts their day to Noriko, stretching from Atami to Shige's to Ueno Park. In contrast to her husband's reminiscence, she tells Noriko she should not hold onto the past but should think about her future and remarry. Tomi (mistakenly) assumes her daughter-in-law's faithfulness to the memory of her son and admonishes her to think more of herself in the future. This is paralleled by Shukichi making excuses ("There are too many people in Tokyo") for his regrets about their remaining Tokyo son. A delicate irony is summoned here, which then lurches into slapstick when Ozu cuts back to Shige, awakened by the police bringing home her besodden father with an uninvited guest. She is furious, because she has been taught a lesson, undermined by the unexpected return of her father's "fighting spirits."

Morning, Day 7, finds the old couple leaving Tokyo, capped by a hangover and Tomi's premonition. Day 8, on which Tomi falls ill en route, is recounted on Day 9 by the younger son, Keizo. On Day 9 the couple is resting at Keizo's in Osaka. These abbreviations are more typical of the truncations and postponements of the first four days in Tokyo when the old couple's presence so disrupts the routines of their children and grandchildren. This initial period in Tokyo concludes with Shige's insistence that "we can do nothing for them here," immediately followed by the unpleasant evening in Atami.

The structural perfection of Ozu's chronopsychological time is matched by playful uses of space and place. The metonymic and retrospective use of Ueno Park is an in-joke based on a simple attribution. We accept it as Ueno Park because it has been so designated by Tomi after the fact, not because it has been specially announced. Instead, it is obliquely hinted at by the reference to homelessness and by the almost surreptitious tracking shot. Similar functions are assigned to the signs designating the Hirayama clinic and the Ulala salon, which are linked in their suggestion of shopkeeper status and accompanying economies of proprietors living on site. There is little separation between living and working spaces, as in the scene in which Shukichi and Numata flop drunkenly into barber chairs to the horror of Shige sleeping on tatami a few feet away. At the more "professional" Koichi's and Shige's, there is hardly any distinction between daily life and working space, with family members either helping with the business (such as Koichi's wife, Fumiko) or trying to stay out of the way (such as Koichi's older son, Minoru). Only Noriko, the "office lady," enjoys a complete separation between work and domestic life.

Even on the first night, the old couple remark that Koichi's neighborhood is not such a *nigiyaka* area, which means "bustling place." While the subtitles emphasize the far-flung, suburban location of Koichi's place with the couple's subsequent remarks on how far it is from Tokyo station, the term *nigiyaka* especially signals expectations of a metropolitan, thriving prosperity. Already then, the splintering of parental expectations from offspring reality has begun in the differentiation of central Tokyo from outlying areas, corresponding to zones of abundance and those of frugality. They have no idea where they are, but they also know where they are not. The old couple is adrift geographically and also cut loose from their imagined Tokyo of prosperity and attraction.

Noriko takes the old couple out for sightseeing on Day 4. This is a displaced event, postponed from the first morning of their arrival and curtailed from the original plan to go with Koichi's whole family. It is a consolation outing, and as with Ueno Park, we are shown only a fragment of the sights and sounds of Tokyo. This sequence is clearly a parody of generic, tourist views of the city, but still, it is a location sequence, which is rare in Japanese film and rarer still in Ozu. Like Koichi's frustrated boys, we have been cued to anticipate this trip, and when the tour guide on the bus promises "the history of this great city," we expect to see more than just a few indifferent shots. The saccharine cheerfulness of tourist music also establishes a programmatic expectation. The guide mentions the magnificent Chiyoda Castle, but Ozu delivers only a single perfunctory long shot. Instead, he seems more interested in the "rubbernecking" movements of the tourists, who swivel their heads to and fro according to the directions of the guide.

Later, Noriko points out where Koichi and Shige live from atop a high building, though we are never privy to the same view. Instead, Ozu cuts to a different, generic skyline shot with the Diet building in the background (Figure 23), followed by another shot of a shabby tenement building (*danchi*) (Figure 24). This would indicate a rich–poor contrast, a cliché of urban representation – but instead this is revealed to be Noriko's building. An anticipated shot-to-shot relation of contrast becomes one of contiguity: a stranger folding clothes (Figure 25) turns out to be Noriko's neighbor (Figure 26). A symbolic representation of the city ("the theme of rich vs. poor") gives way to a material inscription of personal space ("here is Noriko's place"). To keep his audience on guard, Ozu makes fun of canonical, predigested views and clichés of Tokyo that are characteristic of tourism. Taking obvious delight in its deviousness (*zurui*), Ozu's Tokyo is a trickster, a straw woman set up to be sabotaged. The trickery returns us to the old couple's experience of Tokyo as a place too big and slippery to be grasped, a constantly shifting shape amorphous in space and sliding in time.

EDOKKO

Tokyo Story doesn't initially strike one as a very trick-sterish film, but as we have seen, Ozu shrewdly juggles characterization and structure to deliver a comic delicacy in the guise of filial piety. Here we should take stock of the lineage of this trope of urban guile, Edokko, having to do with the transfer of influence between classes, specifically from the exalted samurai to the lowly *chonin*, or "townsman." This in turn relates to the differences between Ozu's generations. Consider the various connotations of Edokko ("child of Edo," technically a third-generation Tokyoite), a venerable stereotype dating from the seventeenth century. Many of Ozu's films, especially his early work, show an affinity for the brash, vulgar enthusiasms of Edokko characters, as in the Kihachi *mono* of *Dekigokoro* (*Passing Fancy*, 1933) and *Ukigusa monogatari* (*A Story of Floating Weeds*,

FIGURE 23

FIGURE 24

FIGURE 25

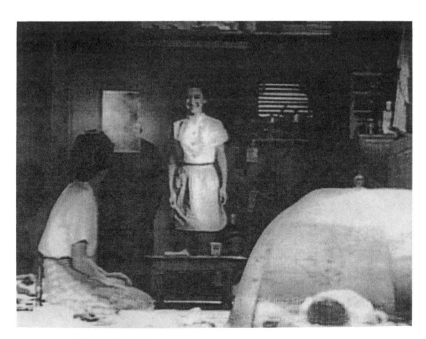

FIGURE 26

1934). The Kihachi character, a modern variety of Edokko, was based partly upon Ozu's own father and other men he met growing up in Fukagawa.[7] And while urban historians are careful to distinguish between the pre-earthquake (1923) Edokko and modern Tokyo-jin, images and inscriptions of Edokko live on in characteristically Japanese forms of superimposition. The stylistically sedate *Tokyo Story* is a cunning invocation of this distinction between unruly ancestor and contemporary poise – only to befoul its pretensions to respectability.

Indeed, Edokko has ceased to be merely a popular culture icon and has been a serious research program for some time. Paul Waley bemoans the way it has acquired a mystique:

> The whole business of the Edokko badly needs rescuing from the fustian research of the academics and the antiquarian mentality of the sentimentalists. For it is undoubtedly true that a special approach to life developed in Edo among the townspeople, an approach that was based inevitably on the bedrock of communal living in the backstreet slums. It was nourished by the citydweller's sense of style (*iki*) and chic (*sui*), and his wit, which expressed itself in a love of comic verse, whether whimsical, satirical, or downright ribald. And it was starved and then again replenished by the Edokko's proverbial and endemic inability to hold onto his money from one day to the next.[8]

A series of huge conflagrations in the mid-seventeenth century periodically flared up over the next two centuries (nearly a hundred of them by 1868)[9] and was associated with a typical, swaggering Edokko figure: the *tobi*, or fireman:

> Among the most celebrated heroes of the common man in Edo were the firemen. Flamboyantly tattooed with dragons – a beast associated with water in Japan and thus with firefighting – these noble tough guys were sent to put out the "Flowers of Edo" by displays of derring-do. They would climb to impossible heights on bamboo ladders, passing heavy buckets of water along a human chain with great acrobatic skill. These once indispensable skills have since been replaced by more

FIGURE 27
Courtesy of the Peabody Essex Museum, Salem, Massachusetts.

modern methods, but they are still practiced every year at the firemen's festival in Tokyo. The ladder-climbing, bucket-juggling, death-defying acts are literally a circus of work[10] [Figure 27].

The fires were so destructive, and so disruptive of established hierarchies and bureaucratic procedures, that they were known as "the flowers of Edo." They were combustible in two senses. These "flowers" bloomed not only in heat and light, but in large brawls as well, because neighboring gangs of firefighters often clashed over jurisdiction, resources, and postconflagration disputes about responsibility – hence the saying "Kaji to kenka wa Edo no hana da" (Fires and fights are the flowers of Edo), and the corresponding association of intermittent disaster and lawlessness.[11]

It is worth remembering why Edo was established in 1590 by the Tokugawa shogunate: as the seat of centralized authority over the whole of Japan, the Edo-based shogunate subjected provincial *daimyo* to a strict system of alternate-year residence in the capital called *sankin kotai*. Edo was initially a garrison town, a colonial outpost full of grizzled, homesick warriors (two-thirds men, 70 percent samurai) forced to leave family and most of their retainers behind.[12] Reluctantly, Edo became their second home. As the country stabilized and Edo grew, so did the need for nonmilitary services (clerical, mercantile, educational, cultural, entertainment), and Edo developed neighborhoods and practices that attenuated the hegemony of the Tokugawa, and of the samurai class generally. The *tobi* and the flowers of Edo, then, contributed to the "choninization" of Edo: "the appropriation of the space, institutions, and cultural motifs of the city by its merchants and artisans at the expense of the government and the ruling samurai status group."[13] At the same time provinces all over Japan underwent gradual "Edofication" due to the constant traffic to and from the Shogun's castle. A colony of provincial samurai under enforced residence in the capital had the ultimate effect of spreading a distinctive metropolitan culture out over the whole country. But this was less a samurai culture than a hybrid, thanks to a mixture of classes and occupations jostling cheek by jowl in the Edo firebreaks and pleasure quarters.[14] This is the source of the easy, maternal acceptance of the Edo *katagi* described by Kojiro in the epigraph.

One of the earliest and best-loved Edokko stories is the early-eighteenth-century *Hizakurige* (*Shank's Mare,* by Ikku Jippensha), a rambling yarn about a pair of fast-talking, free-spending Edo townsmen walking the Tokaido road to Kyoto. Their adventures with provincial bumpkins (*onobori san*), both rustic and shrewd, commemorate a jaunty cock-of-the-walk mien that projects a typical Edokko pragmatism. The periodic destruction and chaos of Edo fires encouraged such attitudes, and hastened the renegotiation of land use and conflict arbitration as fast as it necessitated reconstruction of urban neighborhoods.[15] The flowers of Edo therefore represent a principle of change and ephemerality – of precedents as well as structures – and they also cannot be dissociated from the steady trickle of influence from the samurai to the townsmen, especially merchant, classes (*chonin*).

The firefighting *tobi* were not the only heroes celebrated in the Edokko archetype; "Three Men of Edo" consisted of the Danjuro line of kabuki actors and the wharfmen of the Tsukiji fishmarket, as well as the raffish *tobi*.[16] It should be clear, I hope, that Edokko has little to do with samurai, except insofar as these grim exiles formed the authoritarian background to the shifting consolations of "the floating world": pleasure quarters, *sumo* stables, kabuki and puppet theaters, woodblock prints, and pulp fiction. The melancholy background of *ukiyo* (floating world) must also be acknowledged, as in this gloss on *Sozoro monogatari* (*Idle Tales,* 1641) that contains the first use of the term:

> To sing a song, to drink wine, to console yourself by being carried away while afloat, not to be worried about the last penny you spent – and not to allow your heart to sink holding it like a gourd in the water. That's the way to live in this floating world.[17]

Far from a sense of Buddhist resignation, Saikaku's lugubrious fatalism here is best taken with a grain of salt, coming from the author of the ribald *Life of an Amorous Man* and *Five Women Who Loved Love.* The lusty vitality of Boys' Day *koinobori* is more in keeping with *ukiyo* and the subsequent rise of *chonin bunka* (townsman culture) in the mid-eighteenth century: " 'The *Edokko* is like the carp-shaped streamer blowing in May [*koinobori*]; a real big mouth, yes, but nothing at all inside.' "[18] Edokko therefore suggests bluster and illusion, craft and exchange, if not charlatanism, a character and "a culture of movement and performance (*kodo bunka*)."[19] This is movement of a flowing, historical kind as well.

The samurai will always be with us as an anachronistic emblem of feudal loyalty, but the Edokko is as current as the latest Tora-san serial. Tora-san is "the archetypal Edokko, the Tokyo cockney, happy-go-lucky but sharp-witted, flamboyant but down to earth, and always on the losing end."[20] Like the feckless Kita and Yaji of *Hizakurige*, Tora-san takes definition from his dealings with country people all over Japan (and even abroad) in his peripatetic wanderings as the lovable *tekiya*, itinerant hawker.

Less sentimental twentieth-century incarnations of Edokko include Natsume Soseki's *Botchan* (*The Young Master*, 1906), a stubborn Tokyo chauvinist who finds himself a schoolteacher and the butt of jokes in the wilds of Shikoku; Nagai Kafu's *The River Sumida* (1903), which evokes the sensations of old Tokyo with language that is almost palpable, conjuring visions and smells of Edo that already by the turn of the century were ghosts; the more stark, "photographic" evocation of post-earthquake modern Tokyo in Kawabata's stylish *The Asakusa Crimson Gang* (1929–30) inspired Ozu to make at least two *yotomono* (hoodlum) pictures, *Hogaraka ni ayume* (*Walk Cheerfully*, 1930) and *Hijosen no onna* (*Dragnet Girl*, 1933).[21]

Ozu delighted in the transformations of modern Tokyo but, characteristically, never quite released his hold on the old low city (*shitamachi*). He was born and raised in Fukagawa, across the river from Shibamata, the neighborhood of Tora-san and his world. Here he grew up in typical *chonin* fashion, surrounded by lively back streets, small shopkeepers, sushi shops, and teahouses. Between the ages of ten and twenty, however, he was sent to Matsuzaka, near Nagoya, where he was horribly spoiled by his mother, like the pampered Matsuzaka beef cows whose massaged, sake-fed flesh is known far and wide. "All through his life he was her little boy," says Tadao Sato, even when little Yasujiro periodically returned to Tokyo to visit his father, who ran a fertilizer business.[22] Always a careless student, Ozu somehow graduated but, Botchan-like, found himself a schoolteacher in a backwoods town where he stayed, drinking heavily, until being called back to Tokyo by his father. Shortly afterward, in 1923, he found a job in Shochiku's Kamata studio.

One reason Ozu did badly in school was that, aside from overall unruliness, he was expelled at age seventeen from the Matsuzaka school dormitory for sending a love letter to an attractive junior student.[23] This had a lasting impact on his love life. Subsequently, he was allowed to take classes but had to live at home with his mother, who could not discipline him. Instead of studying, Ozu went to the movies. While Ozu was attracted to various women when he went to Shochiku, he was painfully shy and never converted his attraction into any serious gestures of courtship. Noda Kogo, Ozu's writing partner, remembers how his mother would joke about being a stand-in for Yasujiro's wife and Ozu, in turn, would call her "an ideal mother."[24] In any case, he never married and lived with his mother until her death in early 1962. He followed her in 1963.

It is plain that Ozu's mother functioned as a surrogate wife for him. She looked after him (*mendo miru*) in the way a traditional Japanese wife would have. To some extent this is understandable in Japan, where women's sexuality often assumes maternal forms and the nuclear family is not the sacred cow that it is in the West. Still, in his work as preeminent director of home dramas, Ozu is surprisingly indifferent to romance and marriage in comparison with filial relations. In Ozu's late films, a young woman's marriage prospects are far more important for the forsaking of her parents, particularly her father, than for her own marital relationship. For a man who grew up without a father, spoiled by his mother in his most formative years, Ozu is obsessed with father figures (e.g., *Chichi ariki* [*There Was a Father*, 1942]; *Kohayagawa-ke no aki* [*The End of Summer*, 1961]; *Samma no aji* [*An Autumn Afternoon,* 1962]). For someone who never had his own family, Ozu is a gifted director of small children, from his earliest work with Tokkan Kozo in 1929 to *Ohayo* (*Good Morning*), the 1959 "remake" of the delightful *Umarete wa mita keredo* (*I Was Born, But...,* 1932). For an indifferent student who never went to college, Ozu made wonderful, highly irreverent student comedies (*Daigaku wa deta keredo* [*I Graduated, But ...,* 1929]; *Rakudai wa shita keredo* [*I Flunked, But...,* 1930]; *Wakaki hi* [*Days of Youth,* 1929]). Similarly, Ozu's characterization of Tokyo relies more on its effects on the old folks at home (a trope of hysteron–proteron) than on a direct presentation of those like himself who live by its rhythms and dictates.

In *Tokyo Story,* Ozu perfectly realizes the bewilderment of provincials confronted by the big city, not because he himself went through such travails, but because he considered himself Edokko, child of the city. Ozu understands the enchantment of novelty, of bright lights, of alluring images because he surrendered himself to its promises, fully aware of his familial and educational compromises. Although this story is primarily about the old couple's journey to Tokyo, their children's trade-offs, compromises, and adjustments drive the action. What makes *Tokyo Story* seem prototypical is that the children's amputation from rural *furusato* (hometown) to their grafting onto city life is so complete, so inevitable, so fated. Even Noriko, who is most sensitive to the ringing of generational changes, is an urban fait accompli. Unlike the indignation Kyoko shows toward Shige, the serenity of Noriko's (and Ozu's) acceptance of life's disappointments is proof of her embrace of city life. The point, however, is not to read biographical details into Ozu's films but to look at Ozu's vaunted "traditionalism" in a new way.

It is commonplace to regard Ozu's work as an extended, exquisite elegy to the traditional Japanese family. But in reality, his films' hypertraditional style and characterization are a compensatory imagination for a reality Ozu never had and urban Japanese have long lost. This is why the generational expectations of *Tokyo Story*'s parents and children are so incompatible. Shukichi and Tomi arrive in Tokyo armed with visions of old Edo and of their children prospering in a new frontier of urban promise. Instead they find their children scrimping and struggling to get by in places generically sub-urban, without personality or charm. Anticipating modernity, they do not expect such graceless, drab mediocrity from their children, but they come to perceive that this is modern Tokyo. Nor do they expect such old-fashioned, enthusiastic kindness from their daughter-in-law Noriko. Their fantasies are dashed on the rocks of modern Tokyo, but new possibilities of affiliation arise. Shige and Koichi, for their part, are fooled by their father's reversion to his old drinking tricks. Shukichi's inebriated delusions take him back to old times of patriarchal authority, but to his family these are childish, atavistic, and painful. Still, they serve as a lesson to the imperious Shige.

The bond between Noriko and Tomi is a commutation of the truncated filiality between Shige and her parents. In addition, a role reversal occurs between mother and daughter when Noriko takes charge of caring for her mother-in-law and gives her money. Noriko becomes to Tomi as Tomi once was to Shige. At the same time a reversal of father–daughter roles occurs when drunken Shukichi behaves like a spoiled brat toward his daughter. This echoes the tantrums thrown by Koichi's boys earlier in the film when they are denied their outing. Noriko, however, is the only one who seems (self) aware of the transfer of allegiances from *ie*, the extended family to synthetic city pursuits. She understands and accepts the exchange of traditional kinship for hybrid affiliations of work, school, and amusement. In comprehending the transitional moment, the movement from natal affiliation to urban association, from Edokko to Tokyo-jin, she does not judge, but accepts the inevitability of change. She is a transitional, maternal figure herself in the acceptance of traditional motherhood's obsolescence. In this she hastens the emergence of the city as a replacement for the receding traditional mother, and this is what makes her paradoxical.

The ultimate trick belongs to Tomi, the mother, whose unexpected, but not unforeseen death confounds both generations. The modern city, whose "children" now include those who once were Tomi's, swallows up her cheerful stoicism and forces the family to recombine into a new city–country balance. It is easy to imagine Shukichi and Kyoko, the youngest daughter, continuing life together until the issue of her marriage, another prototypical Ozu dilemma, comes up (e.g., *Banshun* [*Late Spring*, 1949]; *Akibiyori* [*Late Autumn*, 1960]; *Samma no aji* [*An Autumn Afternoon*, 1962]). Not long after Tomi's funeral, however, the city children hurry back to their city lives, plainly exchanging their family kinship for their Tokyo–Osaka loyalties. The centripetal, metropolitan kinship bound by images has taken over those bound by blood or proximity. In the fact that Tokyo, the voracious mother of all cities, has taken Tomi, the mother of *Tokyo Story*, we see the cost of new affiliations of image and perception. We see dreams of migration, progress, and prosperity exchanged for disillusioning realities of modern urban survival. Yet these realities are inscribed in singularly inviting forms. The mother of *Tokyo Story* succumbs to Tokyo itself, as Tokyo serves as maternal replacement for her daughter. As for the daughter-in-law, Tokyo does not replace, but coexists with her memory of traditional filial piety, and she returns to Tokyo with some regrets. But in this film at least, there is little chance that she will give up her metropolitan life. For her, as for Ozu himself, Tokyo comes to be endowed with maternal meaning, even though it means a loss of more organic ties. In this sense Tokyo is Ozu's mother too.

NOTES

1. Yuichiro Kojiro, "Edo: The City on the Plain," in *Tokyo Form and Spirit* (Minneapolis / New York: Walker Art Center / Harry Abrams, 1986), 53.
2. I say the city was "inscribed" to indicate the additional meanings strategically furnished by the film medium, rather than a merely reproductive view implied by "represented." See also Donald Richie, "Attitudes toward Tokyo on Film," in *A Lateral View: Essays on Contemporary Japan*, rev. ed. (Tokyo: Japan Times, Ltd, 1991), 185–95.

3. For an in-depth discussion of Edward Yang's *Terrorizer* (*Kong bu fen zi,* 1986) see Fredric Jameson, "Remapping Taipei," in *The Geopolitical Aesthetic: Cinema and Space in the World System* (Bloomington: Indiana University Press, 1992), 114–57.

4. I am indebted to Henry D. Smith II's "Tokyo as an Idea: An Exploration of Urban Thought Until 1945," *Journal of Japanese Studies* 4:1 (Winter 1978): 45–80, for the notion of trickster Tokyo, in relation to his discussion of Kawabata's *Asakusa Kurenaidan* (*Asakusa Crimson Gang*).

5. This may seem inordinately cruel but to a Japanese audience, according to Sato Tadao, Shige's callousness is probably taken as a joke, the stuff of satire rather than characterization. This adds to the referential and didactic dimension of the film, citing a pressing contemporary problem of the 1950s, as in the title of a popular book called *Children Who Do Not Look After Their Parents.* Tadao Sato, *Ozu Yasujiro no geijutsu* (Tokyo: Asahi Shimbunsha, 1979), 2:169; David Bordwell, *Ozu and the Poetics of Cinema* (Princeton, NJ: Princeton University Press, 1988), 330, 333; see also Hasumi Shigehiko, *Kantoku Ozu Yasujiro* (Tokyo: Chikuma Shobo, 1992).

6. Paul Waley, *Tokyo Now and Then: An Explorer's Guide* (New York: Weatherhill, 1984), 151–60.

7. Bordwell, *Ozu and the Poetics of Cinema,* 249.

8. Waley, *Tokyo Now and Then,* xxvii–xxviii.

9. Ibid., xxiv.

10. Ian Buruma, "Work as a Form of Beauty," in *Tokyo Form and Spirit,* 137.

11. William W. Kelly, "Incendiary Actions: Fires and Firefighting in the Shogun's Capital and the People's City," in *Edo and Paris: Urban Life and the State in the Early Modern Era,* ed. James L. McClain, John M. Merriman, and Ugawa Kaoru (Ithaca, NY: Cornell University Press, 1994), 310–31.

12. Kojiro, "Edo," 40.

13. James L. McClain, "Edobashi: Power, Space, and Popular Culture in Edo," in *Edo and Paris,* 127.

14. See Henry D. Smith II, "Tokyo and London: Comparative Conceptions of the City," in *Japan, A Comparative View,* ed. Albert Craig (Princeton, NJ: Princeton University Press, 1979), 49–99. Especially pertinent are Smith's citations of both England and Japan as "worlds without walls" (Lewis Mumford) and Tokyo specifically as the only capital with an " 'empty center,' a " 'sacred void' ": (*le rien sacre,* Roland Barthes), 68–70.

15. "Tokyo ticks over at a fast pace, and it often has little time to spare

for things of the past. Addresses, like buildings, have a habit of disappearing or changing," writes Waley (*Tokyo Now and Then,* xiii). The wartime firebombing and postwar reconstruction of Tokyo, then, accelerated a process already in place since the seventeenth century, dropping "flowers" even more destructive than those of calamity, arson, or earthquake. For a good, photogenic account of modern Tokyo see Roman Cybriwski, *Tokyo: Changing Profile of an Urban Giant* (London: Belhaven Press, 1991).

16. Kelly, "Incendiary Actions," 325.
17. Kojiro, *Tokyo Form and Spirit,* quoting Asai Ryo, 49.
18. Ibid., 48.
19. Kelly, "Incendiary Actions," citing Henry D. Smith, 327.
20. Waley, *Tokyo Now and Then,* 272.
21. Bordwell, *Ozu and the Poetics of Cinema,* 197. Smith, "Tokyo as an Idea."
22. Donald Richie, *Ozu* (Berkeley: University of California Press, 1974), 193.
23. Ibid., 195–6.
24. " 'When I visited them, she would make jokes such as, "Now Mr. Noda that you have taken the trouble of coming, and that Yasujiro's wife is unfortunately again absent, please content yourself with an old woman like myself" ' " (ibid., 193–4).

4   Buddhism in *Tokyo Story*

     Early attempts to link Ozu's films with Zen Buddhist aesthetics have been joined by later efforts to link his work with traditional Japanese art forms, many of which were inspired by Zen.[1] David Bordwell's objection to the early critiques – that they were too general and failed to take into account that Japanese aesthetics are varied and that Buddhism has changed its emphasis throughout Japanese history – is only partly convincing.[2] True, the aesthetics of Buddhism in Japan have changed with history, but its artifacts remain, as do its basic philosophical contours, which even today influence thought, behavior, and institutions in Japan. Ronald Philip Dore lists various "elements of Buddhist thought . . . so thoroughly absorbed into Japanese culture that they no longer depend on Buddhist institutions for their perpetuation" – among them, "the high value placed on the state of non-self," certain aesthetic values related to Zen, and a "fatalistic determinism emphasizing the necessity of resigned acceptance of one's lot."[3]

     Bordwell's insistence that Ozu evinced little interest in Buddhism is likewise only partly true. During his war service in China, Ozu is reported to have asked a Chinese monk to write the Chinese character *mu* for him. *Mu* is an aesthetic term meaning "void," an emptiness that is nevertheless full of possibilities, such as the empty spaces in a traditional ink-brush painting or the spaces between the branches and flowers in an *ikebana* arrangement. Ozu is said to have kept the monk's painting all his life, and his tombstone in the Zen temple Engakuji in Kita-Kamakura bears the single character *mu* as his only epitaph.[4] Clearly he had a reverence for Zen aesthetics, at the very least.

True, Ozu is quoted as eschewing any Zen influence on his work: "[Foreign critics] don't understand – that's why they say it is Zen or something like that."[5] The full quote, however, reads, "They cannot understand the life of salaried men, ephemerality, and the atmosphere outside of the story at all. That's why they say it is Zen. . . ."[6] Not only is ephemerality (*mujo*) a Buddhist concept, but Ozu's dislike of having his work labeled as such is itself Zen-like. "The basic position of Zen is that it has nothing to say, nothing to teach," writes Alan Watts.[7] If asked, Ozu was quick to head off any discussion of meaning in his films. According to Donald Richie, he insisted that trains frequently appeared in his work because he liked them, then added, "I also like whales."[8] Yet whales never appear in Ozu's films, while trains and train sounds abound, providing a rich symbolic and evocative text. Obviously, Ozu's liking something was no grounds for its inclusion in his films, yet he refused to discuss other possibilities. To do so would undoubtedly have spoiled the immediacy, what Richard Pilgrim calls the "suchness," of the images. "[Zen arts] . . . symbolize nothing beyond themselves," writes Pilgrim, while another writer insists, "Zen culture's primary lesson is that we should start trying to experience art and the world around us rather than analyzing them."[9]

Apart from *Banshun* (*Late Spring*, 1949), which is almost a catalog of traditional Japanese arts, and the wartime *Chichi ariki* (*There Was a Father*, 1942),[10] no Ozu film begs to be looked at in terms of its links to Buddhism more than *Tokyo monogatari* (*Tokyo Story*, 1953). The film begins and ends in Onomichi, whose hills, from which the frequent shots of the harbor were photographed, are filled with more than thirty temples and shrines. The film begins with a shot of the harbor, which fore-grounds a large stone lantern not far from the ferry docks. A subsequent shot in toward the hills shows the Jodo temple, an Onomichi landmark founded by Prince Shotoku, who in the seventh century fostered the growth of Buddhism in Japan. The film's protagonists, Shukichi and Tomi, apparently live near Jo-doji, because after Tomi's death, Shukichi stands in an open area in front of Jodoji and looks out at the sea, flanked by other stone lanterns. This view from Jodoji is remarked on in Tokyo by former Onomichian Mrs. Hattori, who says, "We used to enjoy the view from the temple." That the elderly couple live next door to the temple is confirmed by a later shot of Shukichi tending his garden with Jodoji in the background. The small temple surrounded by a wall that appears in the fifth shot of the opening montage is also part of Jodoji, and Jodoji is the site of Tomi's funeral.[11]

In addition to the temple images associated with Onomichi, small Buddhist images are imbedded in the garden wall of the Onomichi house and appear in every shot in which the garden serves as background. In the final shots of Shukichi sitting alone in his house, these images hover in the background like the guardians they are no doubt intended to be. In addition, Bud-dhist sounds accompany Tomi's funeral: the reciting of prayers, the reading of sutras, and the beating of a wooden drum, which so disturbs the youngest son, Keizo.

Insofar as it still functioned in the everyday life of most Japa-nese in the 1950s, Buddhism was usually confined to the con-ducting of funerals and preserving the memory of the dead. In the household *butsudan* (shrine) tablets (*ihai*) were kept, which bore the names of those who had died within the lifetime of those still living; pictures of the deceased might accompany the tablets. Consequently, the emphasis on Buddhist artifacts in the Onomichi scenes serves to underscore the theme of death, cen-tral to the film, and to locate it within Onomichi, the place where Tomi dies.

This is not to say that, for Ozu, Tokyo or Atami is in contrast to Onomichi, somehow the locus of life. The Tokyo scenes are always introduced by industrial smokestacks, and while the Atami sequences are introduced and concluded with peaceful shots of the sea, these are compromised by the noise and tawdriness of the spa's clientele, city office workers.

Because Buddhist temples cater to the cult of ancestors, "it is the household which is the traditional and fundamental social unit of Buddhism."[12] Associating Onomichi with Buddhist practices, therefore, underscores it as the seat of traditional family life, in contrast to Tokyo, where both family ties and Buddhist observances are more likely to be neglected, particularly by newcomers. "Since we've moved here we haven't bothered to get a new *butsudan* or new *ihai* or anything . . . I'm ashamed to say," replied an informant in Dore's classic study of a Tokyo ward.[13] Keizo's discomfiture during his mother's funeral, tied to his regret at having paid too little attention to her in her later life, relates to this association of Buddhism with the family unit. The drumming, which seems to carry his mother farther away with each beat, reminds Keizo of his neglected duty.[14]

In the film, Onomichi, a provincial backwater on the one hand, comes to stand for all that is good, stable, and ongoing in the Japanese tradition. In a similar vein, the authors of the 1959 *Village Japan* wrote of their subjects, "The people of Niike are sober, responsible, and religious; their religion does not bring about their sobriety, but it comforts and reassures them of order in the world."[15] Tomi's death is sad, yet it is not jarring like the industrial pollution of Tokyo, the grandchildren's rude behavior, or the noisy office workers in Atami. It is part of a natural cycle, which Ozu invokes throughout the film but which reposes most naturally in Onomichi. The opening shots of the harbor and the sounds of chugging boats (Figure 28), children walking to school (Figure 29), and a passing train all suggest this. The recurring stone lanterns, often associated with the souls of the dead, connect these symbols of transience and passage to Buddhism, either the Buddhist escatology of transience or its connection to death, which amounts to the same thing[16] (Figures 30 and 31).

FIGURE 28

FIGURE 29

FIGURE 30

After Tomi's death similar shots are reprised in various combinations at different times of the day.

The notion of "cycle" is invoked in a variety of ways in Buddhist thought. On the one hand, the individual is seen as being caught in an endless cycle of birth, death, and rebirth until enlightenment (*satori*); on the other hand, enlightenment itself can be characterized by the circular. Fifteenth-century noh master Komparu Zenchiku insisted that "extreme enlightenment looks just like non-enlightenment. In the end noh art returns to its original starting point."[17] *Tokyo Story*'s beginning and ending in Onomichi likewise suggest a complete revolution of the life cycle, on the one hand, and possibly the enlightenment invoked by noh, on the other.

Unlike Paul Schrader, I am not convinced that enlightenment and the "transcendent" are attendant on Noriko's tears of regret and frustration near the end of the film. However, a kind of learning occurs between the beginning and the end of the film.

FIGURE 31

Like Dorothy in *The Wizard of Oz*, the parents are inclined to believe "there's no place like home" after experiencing their own disappointments in Tokyo and witnessing those of their friend Numata. They relish returning to the "order in the world" of Onomichi. There, Noriko finally admits her unhappiness and makes way for healing. The rigidity of tradition would bind her to the Hirayama family, but Shukichi, steeped in the Buddhist virtue of compassion and sufficiently aware of the cyclic nature of existence to believe a young, childless widow should not remain unmarried, urges her to break with tradition and re-marry.[18] The "order" that Onomichi represents is, thus, more cosmic than family-oriented or traditional.

Although the trappings of Buddhism in *Tokyo Story* are located in Onomichi, manifestations of Buddhist thought appear throughout the film both within the story and as part of Ozu's film technique. Three characters exhibit the Buddhist virtue of compassion: Tomi, Shukichi, and Noriko.[19] The former two are, of course, from Onomichi, but Noriko lives in Tokyo, expresses her compassion toward the parents in the dingy setting of her urban apartment, and returns to Tokyo with Tomi's watch, doubtless to continue expressing compassion. A lengthy sequence that adds little to the story line suggests, in fact, Noriko's centrality to the film's meaning and moral universe. After learning of Tomi's illness, Koichi's wife, Fumiko, telephones Noriko at work. This is the second time in the film that Fumiko has summoned Noriko to her office telephone, but whereas the first time we simply see Noriko talking on the phone, then asking her boss for a day off, this time a fellow worker answers the phone. Three shots are required before we see Noriko, and two more to get her to the phone. After she hangs up, a sixth shot shows her crossing back to her desk and a seventh holds on her looking sad and thoughtful. Whereas Tomi's illness is compressed into a telegram message and comes as a surprise, much like the father's death in *Kohayagawa-ke no aki* (*The End of Summer*, 1961), seven shots are required to show us Noriko's reaction to the news. While the other siblings are saddened by the news, they seem either helpless (somewhat pathetically, Koichi whistles for his dog while his wife telephones Noriko) or comic (practical Shige suggests taking funeral clothes and hoping not to use them), and none receives the attention accorded Noriko in this seven-shot sequence.

The Buddhist frame of mind most associated with the Tokyo sequences is resignation, what Dore calls "fatalistic determinism," though it is expressed mainly by former Onomichians. Numata's famous "I suppose I should be happy. Nowadays some young men would kill their parents without a thought. Mine at least wouldn't do that" is echoed by Shukichi and Tomi during their Osaka stopover. Shukichi reflects, "Children don't live up to their parents' expectations. . . . Let's think that they [ours] are better than most." Tomi responds, "They are certainly better than average. We are fortunate." The fatalism continues into the Onomichi scenes. Noriko reproves the youngest daughter, Kyoko, for being too idealistic when she complains about her siblings' selfishness. "Life is like that," says Noriko. "Everyone looks after their own affairs..." "Isn't life disappointing?" counters Kyoko. "I'm afraid so," Noriko replies.

Dore notes that this resigned acceptance, derived from Buddhism, became increasingly less relevant in Tokyo of the 1950s, "a society which has a growing faith in its own material progress and places increasing emphasis on the possibility and desirability of getting on."[20] Indeed, the older siblings allow themselves little time for mourning as they hurry back to their busy lives in Tokyo.

Yet his resignation in mourning shows Shukichi at his most sublime. Immediately after his wife's passing, he walks out to a landing in front of Jodoji and observes the dawn. Declining to mention his sorrow, he comments on the sunrise to Noriko, who has come to find him. The end of the film shows him sitting alone, sadly but serenely. "You'll be lonely," suggests a neighbor lady in a reprise of the fleeting visit she had made at the beginning of the film when Tomi and Shukichi were packing for their trip to Tokyo. Shukichi nods obligingly. He will be lonely.

Compassion, selflessness, or the state of "nonself" (*muga*) is considered inseparable from wisdom and is related to the same *mu*, or "void," that informs Japanese aesthetics. Many see in Ozu's style a use of empty space similar to *mu* and its corollary in moving space, *ma*. Schrader notes the "voids and silences" in Ozu's films, the silent reception with which characters often greet disappointments, the "one-corner style" reminiscent of Zen painting in some frames, and the "codas," the uncharactered shots that begin and end most sequences.[21]

I have demonstrated elsewhere that Ozu's codas carry thematic and narrative significance.[22] Ozu was fond of tricks and games, and the codas, sometimes difficult to decode, serve to locate upcoming actions and to comment on those locations – as the recurrent smokestacks in *Tokyo Story* comment on Tokyo – and are generally full of symbols of transience and passage – smoke, trains, bridges, and so on – that support Ozu's ever-present theme of life cycle and transience. The sequence in which the parents leave Tokyo is typical. It begins with a shot of a blank train time board – caught just before the letters announcing the new trains and times turn over. We watch as they turn over, announcing a train leaving at 9:00 p.m., presumably the parents' train. There is a cut to a clock on the wall telling us it is 8:25, followed by a long shot of the passengers and signs over doorways pointing the way to trains leaving at 9:00 and 9:30. Finally, we cut to a shot that includes Noriko, the parents (from the front), Koichi, and Shige (from the rear), followed by close shots of a conversation among all of them. Besides emphasizing the passage of time, the references to trains and time tell us that the parents will leave at 9:00, but that they have about half an hour to train time, enough time to chat with the children. Subsequently, there is a cut back to the long shot with the clock, which reads 8:30 – the conversation we witnessed has supposedly taken five minutes – then cuts to a view of Osaka Castle, to wires over train tracks, to a man running along the track to get to work. The man is Keizo, and he soon informs us and a co-worker that his parents have had to stop over because his mother was taken ill. Up to his usual tricks, Ozu has omitted the parents' original stop to see Keizo in Osaka on the way to Tokyo, but includes a surprise visit on the way back, important narratively, as the first visit was not, because it prepares us for Tomi's final illness and death, which follows immediately after the Osaka sequences. Rather than dangling us helplessly in empty space, as the tenor of some coda critiques suggests, Ozu locates us firmly in Osaka with the identifying shot of the castle. We dangle only insofar as we must wait to find out why.

That said, let me return to the original shot of the train time board. When we first see it, it is blank, a literal tabula rasa, the very image of the "void" so beloved in Buddhist aesthetics. There are narrative and symbolic reasons for the shot of the board, but no particular reason for it to start out blank, except as a kind of embodiment of *mu*. Although the codas have narrative significance, Ozu's privileging them over simply following the action of the characters suggests an aesthetic attitude that places the individual as a mere element in the universe, the "void," rather than at the center of it, as in Western, Greco-Roman thought.

The coda linking the parents' bus tour of Tokyo with a trip to a department store observation deck further illustrates this attitude. It consists of six shots:

- a traveling shot from the moving tour bus in which we see the back of Shukichi's head
- a view of the street through the front window of the bus; we see a tram crossing in front of the bus
- a still shot (no longer on the bus) of the department store's front windows with the top of a tram going by in the bottom of the frame
- a low shot of the observation deck of the department store; an outside stairway is visible
- a shot of two flights of these stairs to the observation deck; five or six people are going up or coming down; three of those coming down, barely recognizable because of the camera's distance from them, are Noriko and the parents
- a match cut to a full shot of these three reaching a landing and going to look out over the edge

The trio in the fifth shot are hard to make out, although it eventually becomes clear that they are our characters, but Ozu just as typically showed strangers in such shots, just as he showed strangers in the later train station sequence before cutting to the parents and Noriko. Such treatment suggests that Ozu has simply plucked these characters out of a universe of very similar people, out of the "void" – hence the emphasis on the quotidian in most of his films.

The "void" can, of course, also comment quite literally on the film's story. As Tomi lies dying, Ozu inserts shots of Onomichi at dawn, which include an empty pier, an empty sidewalk (where schoolchildren walked in the opening sequence), and empty train tracks (where a train ran in the opening sequence). Tomi is dead, gone, void. Later Kyoko watches Noriko's train go down these tracks taking Noriko to a new life. But a shot of the empty tracks precedes a return to Shukichi sitting alone in his living room. Everyone save Kyoko has left him, and he must now deal with that void.

In addition, Ozu's editing suggests various aspects of *ma* space. His intricate linking of shots that take us from one place to another, sometimes through graphic matches and frequently, in *Tokyo Story*, by keeping some element of the preceding shot in the subsequent one, is evocative of that aspect of *ma* space known as *hashi*, the bridging of the void. In the sequence just detailed, bits of the tram serve as a link from the tour bus to the department store. *Ma* is a kind of moving *mu*, a void in which time and space interact and define themselves through an action. The frequently empty rooms that characters go in and out of in Ozu's films suggest *ma*. An early sequence in the film in which Fumiko, the wife of the oldest son, Koichi, readies her house for the parents' visit is cut as follows:

- Fumiko sweeping the upstairs tatami rooms; she goes out and comes back while the static camera waits; she goes out again
- match cut to the hallway as she comes in; she cleans and starts to go out right
- shot of another bedroom; Fumiko comes into camera range (from the right; i.e., the camera has crossed the 180-degree line), then goes out again
- shot of the downstairs hallway; the camera remains static as Fumiko comes in, goes out, comes back again
- Match cut to the back tatami room, where her younger son is playing; she goes out; the boy remains
- cut on Fumiko coming into her husband's clinic
- shot of the entrance hallway (*genkan*); the older son comes in and goes out (right) while camera remains static (Figure 32)
- shot of Fumiko in the clinic; the boy comes in (from the right; i.e., the camera has crossed the 180-degree line again), goes out (Figure 33); Fumiko goes out
- match cut to hallway as Fumiko comes in; she goes out; the boy goes out; the camera remains static on the empty hall until Fumiko crosses in front of it and goes out again

The sequence continues in this way for several more shots: characters crisscrossing a space that is, for the most part, privileged

FIGURE 32

FIGURE 33

over their coming and going. In *ma* terms the rooms in the house evoke *susabi,* the empty place where "phenomena appear, pass by, and disappear."[23]

Susabi also means "to play," and there are indications that this tendency in Ozu's films may have its roots as much in Japanese religion as in Ozu's own psychology. There are several instances in the sequence where characters leave a room going in one direction and enter the next room from the opposite direction. It is an old trick, crossing the 180-degree line, frequently found in Ozu's films and one that has generated much attention from critics emphasizing Ozu's iconoclastic tendencies.[24] While Ozu's iconoclasm is clear, there are shades of Zen in his playing with directions. Alan Watts points to the *hosshin,* a type of koan, or Zen riddle, posed to students that begins by sending them off "in the direction exactly opposite to that in which they should look."[25] Such Zen-like confusion is suggested in *Late Spring* when the father's friend Onadera asks which way it is to the sea. He points behind him, and the father replies, no, it is in the opposite direction and points behind himself. Then Onadera asks the direction of the shrine and points to his left. The father says, no, it is this way, and points to his right. However, because Ozu crosses the 180-degree line to show us the father, both men point in the same screen direction (right), adding to the confusion and hilarity of the scene. Onadera goes on to ask about two more directions, both of which he mistakes as he did the others. This sequence is echoed, though without the confusion, in *Tokyo Story* when the parents look out from the landing on the observation tower stairs and Noriko points out where their son Koichi lives, where the daughter Shige lives, and finally, turning and pointing in the opposite direction, where she lives. (Financially and morally she is opposite to the other siblings.) Later on, from another overlook, the mother comments that if she and the father lost one another in Tokyo, they might never meet again.

To what extent Ozu's tricksterism – crossing the 180-degree line, taking us to Osaka when we expect to go to Onomichi –

which abounded in his early films, is related to the Zen koan is, without other evidence, impossible to say, but the mind-set, particularly as he matured, seems similar.[26] Certainly "breaking the rules" was an honored tradition in Japanese art,[27] a source, no doubt, of much that we find startlingly modern in it.

That the *mu* and *ma* of Zen aesthetics permeated Ozu's work there seems no question, though his interest in Buddhism as such was undoubtedly confined to aesthetics. The specific Buddhist attitudes that inhere in his characters, particularly the admirable characters, are among those Dore cites as having become part of Japanese culture generally. But as an overarching motif in *Tokyo Story,* Buddhism is important for its associations with the family and with death. Its artifacts help to distinguish Onomichi from Tokyo, the old from the new, the traditional from the nontraditional. These in turn combine with compassion (*muga,* or nonself) and resignation to distinguish the admirable characters from the less admirable. In doing this, however, the spiritual side of Buddhism bursts the boundaries of the traditional side when Noriko is admonished to leave the family and find her own happiness, and the universality of the ethic and aesthetic is demonstrated.

NOTES

1. See Marvin Zeman, "The Serene Poet of Japanese Cinema: The Zen Artistry of Yasujiro Ozu," *Film Journal* 1:3–4 (Fall–Winter 1972): 62–71; Paul Schrader, *Transcendental Style in Film: Ozu, Bresson, Dreyer* (Berkeley: University of California Press, 1972); Ruth Vasey, "Ozu and the Nō," *Australian Journal of Screen Theory* 7:80 (1988): 88–102; and Kathe Geist, "Playing with Space: Ozu and Two-Dimensional Design in Japan," in *Cinematic Landscapes,* ed. Linda C. Ehrlich and David Desser (Austin: University of Texas Press, 1994), 283–98.
2. David Bordwell, *Ozu and the Poetics of Cinema* (Princeton, NJ: Princeton University Press, 1988), 26–30.
3. Ronald Philip Dore, *City Life in Japan: A Study of a Tokyo Ward* (Berkeley: University of California Press, 1958), 362.
4. Inoue Kazuo, *Ikite wa mita keredo . . . (I Lived, But . . .* ; Tokyo: Shochiku, 1983), a film biography of Ozu.

5. Donald Richie, *Ozu: His Life and Films* (Berkeley: University of California Press, 1974), 256; also quoted in Bordwell, *Ozu and the Poetics of Cinema,* 27).

6. Yamamoto Kikuo, "Postscript," in Paul Schrader, *Seinaru eiga* (Tokyo: Film Art-sha, 1981), 282. The quote was originally printed in *Kinemo Jumpo* (August 1958).

7. Alan Watts, *The Way of Zen* (New York: Pantheon Books, 1957), 160.

8. Richie, *Ozu,* 254.

9. Richard B. Pilgrim, *Buddhism and the Arts of Japan* (Chambersburg, PA: Anima Books, 1981), 5; and Thomas Hoover, *Zen Culture* (New York: Random House, 1977), 228.

10. Bordwell describes the Buddhist elements in *There Was a Father* in some detail, seeing behind them the influence of wartime propaganda (*Ozu and the Poetics of Cinema,* 289–91).

11. Although there are few shots that might positively identify the temple in the funeral scene, Keiko McDonald believes the funeral temple is the temple seen from the harbor in the opening montage, that is, Jodoji, on the basis of the Japanese script, and the Tourist Department in the Onomichi City Hall has confirmed this identification. See McDonald's *Cinema East: A Critical Study of Major Japanese Films* (East Brunswick, NJ: Associated University Presses, 1983), 205.

12. Joy Hendry, *Marriage in Changing Japan* (London: Croom Helm, 1981), 63; see also 232.

13. Dore, *City Life in Japan,* 314.

14. The actual duty to one's parents, so neglected by the children in *Tokyo Story,* is a Confucian virtue, as is the Japanese code of ethics generally, and not a Buddhist virtue, but the circumstances of the Buddhist funeral remind Keizo of this duty.

15. Richard K. Beardsley, John W. Hall, and Robert E. Ward, *Village Japan* (Chicago: University of Chicago Press, 1959), 470.

16. The "birth–destruction cycle, repeated endlessly, is the basis of Japanese eschatology" (Cooper–Hewitt Museum, *MA: Space-Time in Japan,* exh. cat. [New York, n.d.], 16).

17. Pilgrim, *Buddhism and the Arts,* 55.

18. Bordwell calls this "Occupation-tinted liberalism," but here as in both his and Kristin Thompson's critiques of *Late Spring,* "Occupation liberalism" is largely imagined. In Ozu's cosmology, Noriko is a candidate for remarriage only because she is still young and childless. Her niche in the life cycle is akin to that of the unmarried but slightly "old" (late twenties) daughters in *Late Spring* and *Ba-*

kushu (*Early Summer*, 1950). Ozu did not permit those who had passed this rung on the ladder to remarry with grace. Widows and widowers with children were seen as somehow betraying their children if they remarried, and the most admirable of them, those played by Hara or Ryu, do not do so when given the chance. Subsidiary characters who have remarried are treated as comic figures. If anything, the Occupation seems to have stiffened Ozu's resolve to invoke "Japaneseness" – hence the catalog of arts in *Late Spring*. The only film from this period that possibly reflects Occupation values is *Early Summer* with its liberated, Katharine Hepburn–esque heroine. Even so, Ozu fashions her after his own ideals and grounds her independence in solid virtue rather than merely fashionable behavior. See Bordwell, *Ozu and the Poetics of Cinema*, 33; Kristin Thompson, *Breaking the Glass Armor* (Princeton, NJ: Princeton University Press, 1988), 320–6; and Kathe Geist, "Marriage in the Films of Yasujiro Ozu," *East–West Film Journal* 4:1 (December 1989): 47–49.

19. McDonald, *Cinema East*, 204.
20. Dore, *City Life in Japan*, 363.
21. Schrader, *Transcendental Style in Film*, 28–9.
22. Kathe Geist, "Narrative Strategies in Ozu's Late Films," in *Reframing Japanese Cinema*, ed. Arthur Nolletti and David Desser (Bloomington: Indiana University Press, 1992), 92–110.
23. Cooper-Hewitt Museum, *MA*.
24. David Bordwell and Kristin Thompson were the first to make much of this in their original Ozu analysis, "Space and Narrative in the Films of Ozu," *Screen* 17:2 (Summer 1976), 41–73.
25. Watts, *The Way of Zen*, 160.
26. Alain Bergala sees similarities to koan in Ozu's prewar *Passing Fancy* ("Coeur capricieux," *Cahiers du cinéma*, no. 311 [May 1980]: 35).
27. Pilgrim, *Buddhism and the Arts*, 54.

5 **Sunny Skies**

Early on the morning that his wife has just breathed her last, a father (Ryu Chishu) stands at the edge of a wide-open garden, looking out at the sea over the rooftops of the clustered houses. He has slipped away from his house, where his children and relatives are gathered, having hurriedly arrived from Tokyo and Osaka. His daughter-in-law (Hara Setsuko) comes running out and stops beside him. In this scene situated near the end of *Tokyo monogatari* (*Tokyo Story,* 1953), what could the widowed Ryu be thinking? Saying that everyone is waiting, Hara invites him back to the house. Then, out of the blue, the father-in-law mentions that this day, on which his wife's last rites are about to be held, looks like it is going to be hot. Behind them, in fact, stretches a perfectly clear sky. What kind of symbol should one read in this reference to the weather? Is Ryu trying to say that unlike what one would expect, this is the start of a particularly hot day? Or is he saying that, *as always,* this day is going to be a hot one? We can infer from the scene that what we see undoubtedly signals the beginning of another hot day. As usual, it is one of Ozu's sunny mornings. Donald Richie correctly points out that the reference in this scene to weather conditions is by no means uncommon. While observing that "this sort of singular concern with weather is rare, even in Japan, where people always pay attention to the weather," Richie makes the point that one function of references to the weather is their "sharp interruption of scenes of considerable emotional tension." Indeed, there is no question that such references function in that way, but speeches related to weather serve more than the kind of narrative function that Richie observes. This is because the characters in Ozu's works are not merely paying attention to weather in general.

Examples of observations on Ozu's perpetually blue skies abound, from the "It's gonna be a hot one . . ." that begins *Ukigusa* (*Floating Weeds,* 1959), spoken by someone in a very minor role, to the "Ahh, great weather" in whatever film, in whichever scene, repeated in so many places that we forget who said it. No Ozu film made on a predominantly cloudy day exists. Even the clouds to which Sugai Ichiro turns his gaze at a railroad crossing of the Yokozuna Line in *Bakushu* (*Early Summer,* 1951) emphasize the exhilaratingly fine weather. In the scene, a spectacularly clear sky, without a trace of precipitation, spreads forth. The same sky stretches behind the shot that captures Higashiyama Chieko's face, with the camera pointing up at a slight angle, as she mentions a premonition of death while playing with her grandchild in the grass on the riverside.

Of course, when heat is mentioned, there will be some people fluttering fans or men wearing summer kimonos with wet, folded washcloths on their heads. But this is not the damp heat of the rainy season. When it is hot, people and houses always cast distinct shadows; heat is, throughout Ozu's films, an attribute of fine weather. "Existence" in an Ozu film means that everyone inhales the air of a clear, sunny day. Thus, in black-and-white films, the whiteness of a woman's dress, wash hanging on the line, the wall of a house are emphasized, and in color films a blue sky stretches as far as the eye can see. Just as if the Japanese archipelago were not located in a subtropical zone with a rainy season, the light in Ozu's films is almost the same as that in California, with its movie town, Hollywood, or that of an open set in Nice on the Mediterranean. So, in Ozu's films, people *are not paying attention to the weather.* It is in order to assure themselves that they are, without a doubt, in Ozu's world that people say, "Ahh, great weather" and "It's gonna be a hot one." In exceptional cases, when there is rain or a light snowfall, these are almost certainly unlucky omens. In Ozu films, the sky can only be sunny.

At this point, one understands that calling Ozu Yasujiro a *very Japanese* director is a huge mistake. In Ozu's world, not only is there no rainy season, there is not even anything like a season-able shower. In fact, nothing could be further from Ozu's work than the rhetoric referring to the seasons found in haiku poetry. Since Ozu's films never depict delicate seasonal transitions – plum blossoms opening, fallen leaves scattering, frost covering the ground – we cannot say that he is a director sensitive to the so-called expressions of nature. With an almost cruel consistency, Ozu ignores the seasons. Whether it is titled *Higanbana* (*Equinox Flower,* 1958), *Banshun* (*Late Spring,* 1949), *Bakushu* (*Early Summer*), or *Akibiyori* (*Late Autumn,* 1960), no Ozu film has a seasonal context. Or rather, no problems are posed by cold or humidity; from spring to summer to fall, the rainy season is ignored and fine weather continues. And the nights are always moonlit, as in *Late Spring,* where nothing could be further from nocturnal haze than the shadow of the moon that falls on the sliding door at the Kyoto inn.

In the films of Mizoguchi Kenji, for example, fog is an essential theatrical device, and one cannot imagine a Kurosawa film in which rain does not fall. At the opposite pole of the intense heat in *Nora inu* (*Stray Dog,* 1949) is the cold in *The Idiot* (*Hakuchu,* 1951). Things like the nocturnal lyricism of Mizoguchi are uncharacteristic of Ozu. When the director reaches his later period, even characters wearing overcoats become rare and many of the men go to work in open-collared shirts. When *was* the last time we saw a man or woman wearing a muffler in an Ozu film? Ah, yes, in *Ohayo* (*Good Morning,* 1959), people are wearing coats and sweaters. Even so, in no other film is "great weather" muttered as often as it is in this one. Of course, Ryu Chishu does come into Tokyo holding an umbrella to his chest in *Tokyo Story*. But even though such rain gear may be seen at the threshold of a drawing room or hanging in a hall, the type of weather that would require it is almost never depicted.

Still, nothing could be more un-Japanese than Nature without cold and rain. According to Tom Mills, who introduced Ozu's films in Great Britain, there could be nothing stranger than comparing Ozu's works to haiku poetry. When Paul Schrader broaches the subjects of *wabi* (sober, austere refinement) and *sabi* (the grace, charm, or beauty acquired with age) or gives an account of *yugen* (mysterious profundity), or when Donald Richie mentions *mono no aware* (the pathos or transience of things), we are beset by uncomfortable thoughts. Nothing about the light in Ozu's scenes would lead someone to that kind of Japanese aesthetic sense. This atmosphere is not an expression of a subtle world that is for some reason difficult to grasp: under the sunlight of a fine day, everything is already clear. There is nothing as unearthly as the red of the resplendent amaranth in the courtyard of Sugimura Haruko's house in *Floating Weeds,* a film in which very little rain falls. There is no nuance here; the flowers are just red. There is no ambiguity in Ozu's films to blur the outlines of things. He is a broad-daylight director: rather than subtle nuances, he adheres to an excess of clarity. The skies are forbidden to cloud ambiguously; typically, only fine weather is allowed.

But one cannot conclude from this that Ozu's scenes are devoid of subtlety or lacking in poetic sentiment. Ozu is a director who understands how to imbue a scene with poetic sentiment in a bold and brutal way; his is a domain totally different from a Japanese rhetoric based on seasonal words, which people too easily believe to be poetic. Ozu's talent lies in choosing an image that can function poetically at a particular moment by being assimilated into the film, not by affixing to the film the image of an object that is considered poetic in a domain outside the film. Whether or not it is called "poetic" is meaningless. Let us say that the cinematic emotions we experience the instant the film is projected onto the screen are *poetic*. Whatever our conclusions, Ozu avoids steeping the object on the screen in lyricism. Ozu manipulates what we are watching without mediation and *by-passing psychology* by bringing to the surface the condition of the film's being a film. We may assume that this is true of the scene in *Early Summer* in which a commemorative photograph is being taken.

In that sense, I believe Ozu, who repeatedly spoke of the highly acclaimed masterpiece of his later years, *Tokyo Story,* as "the film that tends most strongly toward melodrama," was a master with an extremely objective point of view. We may say that of all his films this one has the greatest impact on the audience through its story. For example, there are no obvious details that excite our emotions, like the commemorative photo in *Early Summer,* the deserted staircase in *Samma no aji (An Autumn Afternoon,* 1962), or the quarrel between the rain-soaked couple that takes place in *Floating Weeds.* Since even the lyricism of the Atami breakwater sequence, considered a "famous scene," can be understood psychologically, the exchange of the elderly couple in this sequence, even compared with the reticence of the glance exchanged by the elderly couple who sit down in the museum garden in *Early Summer,* seems, if anything, too verbal. What Ozu means by melodrama and the limits of film is that *Tokyo Story* is a story told without exposing the compelling features of his own cinematic world.

Nevertheless, *Tokyo Story* is an incredibly moving film. This is because the perfectly clear sky on the morning Higashiyama Chieko is taking care of her grandson and the warm day that will become increasingly sun-drenched are so vividly caught on film. When the death of the elderly mother becomes certain, the camera suddenly pulls away from the drawing room, where the body is laid out to the bright morning outdoors. What one sees then is just an ordinary wharf in the harbor. The camera, in a low position, captures the wharf jutting out to sea in a vertical composition: the sea and the hills, on the opposite side of the dark, backlit roof and its steel pillars that rise to the surface. A "morning atmosphere" permeates the surroundings of the wharf. Though the shot is an extremely short one, it gives a surprisingly clear impression, first of all through the absence of a human form and then by establishing an unobstructed view.

In *Tokyo Story*, the harbor roofs, shown as having great depth, are central to the scene overlooking Onomichi Harbor: these roofs are what accent the composition as a straight horizontal line. Here and in all of the following scenes of the port, we catch sight of those horizontally stretching roofs. The contrast formed by the series of horizontal and vertical compositions is somehow moving.

In the accumulation of various brief shots – around the fishing boats shot from a low position, on the lonely road – nowhere is there a deluge of light. The sole purpose of this scene is to bring to the forefront, literally and with none of the film's characters to witness the sight, the serene atmosphere of early morning. Nevertheless, that indeterminate time and space depicts, beautifully and absolutely, the fact that it is the beginning of a fine, hot day. It is simultaneously the instant when a new day begins and one life ends. This extremely short scene, in just a few shots, depicts the beginning and the end.

Ozu figuratively expresses the fact of Tanaka Kinuyo's prostitution in the relevent scene from *Kaze no naka no mendori* (*A Hen in the Wind*, 1948) by linking skillfully arranged short shots. We might say that the same technique is used to depict Higashiyama Chieko's death. But in the latter case Ozu is portraying both the shift from life to death and the course of ordinary time, that is, the shift from night to day.

This double shift, at once fateful and universal, is conveyed through the dull, dry sensation of the early-morning scene. Compared with the technique used in the house of prostitution scene in *A Hen in the Wind*, the technique in *Tokyo Story* is not just rhetorical verbosity. Nor is it metonymical: the impression of death's unexpectedness and the premonition of hot weather are connected directly to the picture on the screen. Regardless of Ryu Chishu's murmured "Ah, it was a beautiful sunrise," something in the deserted scene of the roofed wharfs exceeds the image that we know as "sunrise." As a metonymical expression of "sunrise," while this scene shows something extra, paradoxically it also gives the impression of a deficiency. Most likely this is because the string of steel pillars, in perspective, that supports the pitch-black roofs embodies something that cannot be understood by the study of Japanese rhetoric based on seasonal words. Because Ozu consistently avoids giving a scene depth through vertical composition, this scene makes us recognize the conversion of Ozu's audacity into something visible. We cannot imagine the scene being an object of Japanese aesthetic study, full as the latter is of those who speak of modesty and restraint. We, the viewers, are amazed and can only stare at this unexpected shot; without allowing this surprise to sink in, the director takes us back to the room where the death of the elderly mother is indisputable. We should be able to perceive Ozu's poetic sentiment in this kind of audacious subtlety. In Ozu's scenes, nothing is saturated in the lyricism of a rhetoric based on seasonal words; as for narrative continuity, he has abandoned, too, the cinematic desire to surprise.

A BROAD-DAYLIGHT DIRECTOR

Among Ozu's series of black-and-white films that almost always take place under sunny skies, *Tokyo Story* is, perhaps, the work in which the impression made by the heat is the most beautifully embedded. That consistent heat is what moves us. From the point of view of typically Japanese reactions to seasonal conditions, this kind of heat should provoke one to mutter about the need for a little rain. But none of the characters in this film does so; it is as if they will accept only heat and clear skies. When Ryu Chishu, having just lost his wife, looks down on Onomichi Harbor and says, "Today'll be another hot one," he appears to be blessing the fine weather. Or we might say that suddenly he is reassured, not having lost sight of the world created by Ozu. Thus, just as it is frequently referred to during the reminiscences on the day of the funeral service for Hara Setsuko's husband in *Late Autumn,* that severe heat is also recollected on the day of Higashiyama Chieko's death in *Tokyo Story.* In *Kohayagawa-ke no aki (The End of Summer,* 1961), too, the day of Nakamura Ganjiro's death, though in autumn, will no doubt be another hot one. The elderly, without exception, breathe their last on a fine day. That Ozu successfully filmed *Tokyo Story*'s scenes of sunny skies and high temperatures in black and white makes it an especially important work. In the color films that follow, the radiance of *Tokyo Story*'s slow-moving scenes is gone.

Even so, though there are few shots of the sky, no other of Ozu's works expresses as cruelly the radiance of sunlight. Watching *Tokyo Story,* we are moved once again by the fact that Ozu is not a gloomy artist, but one permeated by the clarity of broad daylight. Of course, nighttime is not completely absent from his work; in the crime films of his early period, there is graphic gloom and even things that make us gasp. Nevertheless, Ozu is, persistently, a broad-daylight director; a drop of rain rarely falls from his cloudless blue sky. The films in which rain falls unexpectedly or a chill approaches with the nocturnal humidity are moving.

Looking down at the sea, having just lost his wife, Ryu Chishu has not a thought in his mind. In this respect, Ryu is not unique among Ozu's characters; in his films, state of mind, as a rule, does not exist. At that moment, Ryu suddenly and mechanically mentions the heat and the appropriately sunny skies, just as anyone might have done. No deep meaning is intended. This trivial verbal exchange between Ryu and Hara Setsuko in a corner of the garden, though merely ritualistic, is probably more moving than the rather important speech in which she, remaining behind, seems satisfied with her life as it is. This is because there is nothing further from melodrama than Ozu's characters' references to the weather. Such references are not at all theatrical; they bring about a transformation of narrative continuity, play a role similar to a punctuation mark by shifting an episode to the next scene, and perform a literal verbal-exchange function. We might say that, with these exchanges as opportunities, the film *moves*.

As we have just seen, the words exchanged by Ryu and Hara early that morning in the garden are nothing more than a brief, superficial, mechanical, monotonous, and somewhat ritualistic, repetition. "Existence" in nearly all of Ozu's films means that lines like these are being spoken throughout. Nevertheless, the repetition here is a necessity. Preceded by the deserted scene at sunrise, the scene involving Higashiyama Chieko as she lies unconscious, and that which follows of the funeral define, as it were, the boundary between life and death. Everyone, the children who have gathered around their mother's deathbed and, of course, the father, is wearing everyday clothes. As always, Hara Setsuko, who goes to call Ryu in the garden, is wearing a short-sleeved white blouse. Bearing in mind the significance of clothing, we realize that the hour of death until now has been associated with everyday time. And after the two go inside, funereal time begins. Having received a telegram about the mother's illness and having been so indecisive about whether to take mourning clothes when they are about to leave Tokyo, the eldest son and daughter, played by Yamamura So and Sugimura Haruko, take this as an opportunity to wear them. Moreover, their conversation about having to rent mourning clothes from a rental shop takes place just before they leave for Onomichi. These points, too, clarify that the shift from the sunny outdoors to inside space necessitates a change from everyday time to ritualism.

Ritualism here is emphasized by mourning clothes. But true ritualism is not defined by that fact. A scene during the funeral in which every member of the family sits in a line, in the same pose, facing the same direction is ritualistic. Considering this scene, we might examine more thoroughly both the subject of sitting in a line and the tendency for the actors' lines of vision to share the same direction. With voices chanting Buddhist sutras and the sound of a wooden drum reverberating, the family members sit facing, and at an equal distance from, the Buddhist altar, bowing with their gazes turned equally downward. The camera does not face its subjects directly, as it would for a commemorative photograph: Ozu positions the figures so that they are shot diagonally from the side. Of course, there is no frontal view that would make us grasp the meaning of the placement of those attending a ritual of farewell, that is, a funeral. The arrangement of figures is displayed through a series of fragmentary scenes, as was done in almost the same way in the scene of the Buddhist memorial service in *Late Autumn.*

Moreover, as on the day of the funeral in *The End of Summer,* outdoors it is sunny. Ozu, as if trying to make us consent to that fact, has the third son, played by Osaka Shiro, sit to the side by himself. On the occasion of the seventh-year memorial service in *Late Autumn,* the light playing on the surface of the pond, which appears to be surrounded by the temple, is made to reflect on both the opaque and the translucent sliding paper doors. In *Tokyo Story,* expressed in the clear sky that spreads behind the many tombstones caught in Osaka's gaze, the heat and fine weather intervene as essential elements in the farewell ritual. The day of the funeral in *Late Autumn,* too, is hot enough to be recollected seven years later. Within the "existence" created by Ozu, everyone's fate is to die on a hot, sunny, midsummer day. And those present at the funerals and memorial services must wear mourning clothes.

If we consider the depiction of nature and the seasons, we must say that Kurosawa Akira and Mizoguchi Kenji are far more "Japanese" than Ozu. Regardless of the rain and snow that fall in *Floating Weeds* and *Tokyo Twilight,* Ozu's eternally cloudless skies are much more closely connected to the fine weather of California, the land Jean Renoir chose as his retreat from the world, or to the sky of John Ford's Monument Valley. Like the West Coast of California, where the cinema was born, where it grew and matured, the sunny skies of Ozu must be clear as far as the eye can see. His exclusion from the screen of the rainy season, the damp climate unique to Japan, was a choice made in order to insist on a specifically filmic reality. That may be a manifestation of what might be called an antiquarian ambition toward film, an ambition Ozu shared with many directors in his circle. The attraction of night and darkness in films, moreover, was developed under California skies. The light of California, location of the film capital, Hollywood, reappears in Japan. Isn't this characteristic desire of Ozu to be filmic rather than realistic – a desire that is almost reckless – far more important than the influence of the Ozu who, in his early period, was enthusiastic about Hollywood comedies of the silent era and skillfully transplanted several of them into a Japanese climate?

Whatever the case may be, calling Ozu Yasujiro "very Japanese" is based on a lack of understanding of his works. Rather than being confined by that ambiguous phrase, he chose a persistent approach toward film and its limits. And liberated from the ambiguity of outlines, dampness, and shadows, he chose to place in the dry sunlight things and characters that, in their manners and customs, are obviously very Japanese. We would like to acknowledge that choice. Of course, it must be a gesture that simultaneously acknowledges Kurosawa Akira's rain and Mizoguchi Kenji's fog. However, I must point out again how strange it is for Ozu, still a broad-daylight director whether his films are enveloped in rain, snow, or cold, to be called "very Japanese" through the easy solidarity of those who would ignore the screen.

It is foolish to assert that Ozu is an "un-Japanese" director. Even though Ozu, who avoided the world of shadows that made the outlines of things ambiguous, whose sole purpose was to approach the dazzle of midsummer sunlight, is in many ways the opposite of those said to have a "very Japanese" aesthetic sense, he is an unmistakably Japanese artist. Putting ourselves within the "gap" between a film by Ozu and "things characteristic of Ozu," and considering the portrayal of usual movements as a game in his films, we are tempted to experience once again the gap between "things Japanese" and Japan. Just as Ozu is neither solely nor entirely "things characteristic of Ozu," neither must Japan be thought of as consonant with "things Japanese." At the very least, "things characteristic of Ozu" will ensure that his works are not ignored.

TRANSLATED BY KATHY SHIGETA

Filmography

All films, unless otherwise noted, were produced at Shochiku Studios. All films until 1936 were made at Shochiku's Kamata studio; after 1936, the Shochiku productions were made at the Ofuna studio, with one exception noted. Films marked with "vt" are available on video tape, but availability might vary. Films available for rent are marked "16mm" followed by the company that distributes them (NY, New Yorker; FI, Films Inc; K, Kino).

1927

The Sword of Penitence (*Zange no yaiba*)
Screenplay: Noda Kogo, from the film *Kick-in*
Director: Ozu Yasujiro
Director of photography: Aoki Isamu
Cast: Azuma Saburo, Ogawa Kunimatsu, Atsumi Eiko

1928

The Dreams of Youth (*Wakodo no yume*)
Screenplay: Ozu Yasujiro
Director: Ozu Yasujiro
Director of photography: Shigehara Hideo
Cast: Saito Tatsuo, Wakaba Nobuko, Yoshitani Hisao, Matsui Junko

Wife Lost (*Nyobo funshitsu*)
Screenplay: Yoshida Momosuke, from an idea by Takano Ononosuke
Director: Ozu Yasujiro
Director of photography: Shigehara Hideo
Cast: Saito Tatsuo, Matsui Junko, Okamura Ayako, Sakamoto
    Takeshi

Pumpkin (*Kabocha*)
Screenplay: Komatsu Kitamura
Director: Ozu Yasujiro
Director of photography: Shigehara Hideo
Cast: Saito Tatsuo, Hinatsu Yurie, Sakamoto Takeshi

A Couple on the Move (*Hikkoshi fufu*)
Screenplay: Fushimi Akira, from an idea by Kikuchi Ippei
Director: Ozu Yasujiro
Director of photography: Shigehara Hideo
Cast: Watanabe Atsushi, Yoshikawa Mitsuko, Oyama Kenji

Body Beautiful (*Nikutai bi*)
Screenplay: Ozu Yasujiro and Fushimi Akira
Director: Ozu Yasujiro
Director of photography: Shigehara Hideo
Cast: Saito Tatsuo, Iida Choko, Yoshikawa Mitsuko

1929

Treasure Mountain (*Takara no yama*)
Screenplay: Ozu Yasujiro and Fushimi Akira
Director: Ozu Yasujiro
Director of photography: Shigehara Hideo
Cast: Kobayashi Tokuji, Iida Choko, Okamura Ayako

Days of Youth (*Wakaki hi*)
Screenplay: Ozu Yasujiro and Fushimi Akira
Director: Ozu Yasujiro
Director of photography and editing: Shigehara Hideo
Cast: Saito Tatsuo, Matsui Junko, Yuki Ichiro

Fighting Friends, Japanese Style (*Wasei kenka tomodachi*)
Screenplay: Noda Kogo
Director: Ozu Yasujiro
Director of photography: Shigehara Hideo
Cast: Watanabe Atsushi, Yuki Ichiro, Naniwa Tomoko

I Graduated, But. . . (*Daigaku wa deta keredo*)
Screenplay: Aramaki Yoshiro, from an idea by Shimizu Hiroshi
Director: Ozu Yasujiro
Director of photography: Shigehara Hideo
Cast: Takada Minoru, Tanaka Kinuyo, Suzuki Utako

The Life of an Office Worker (*Kaisha-in seikatsu*)
Screenplay: Noda Kogo
Director: Ozu Yasujiro
Director of photography: Shigehara Hideo
Cast: Saito Tatsuo, Yoshikawa Mitsuko, Sakamoto Takeshi

A Straightforward Boy (*Tokkan kozo*)
Screenplay: Ikeda Tadao, from an idea by Nozu Chuji (Noda Kogo,
    Tadamoto Okubo, Ikeda Tadao, Ozu Yasujiro)
Director: Ozu Yasujiro
Director of photography: Nomura Ko
Cast: Saito Tatsuo, Aoki Tomio, Sakamoto Takeshi

1930

An Introduction to Marriage (*Kekkon-gaku nyumon*)
Screenplay: Noda Kogo, from an idea by Okuma Toshio
Director: Ozu Yasujiro
Director of photography: Shigehara Hideo
Cast: Saito Tatsuo, Kurishima Sumiko, Yoshikawa Mitsuko, Takada
    Minoru

Walk Cheerfully (*Hogaraka ni ayume*)
Screenplay: Ikeda Tadao, from an idea by Shimizu Hiroshi
Director: Ozu Yasujiro
Director of photography and editing: Shigehara Hideo
Cast: Takada Minoru, Kawasaki Hiroko, Date Satoko, Sakamoto
    Takeshi

I Flunked, But. . . (*Rakudai wa shita keredo*)
Screenplay: Ozu Yasujiro and Fushimi Akira
Director: Ozu Yasujiro
Director of photography and editing: Shigehara Hideo
Cast: Saito Tatsuo, Tanaka Kinuyo, Ichiro Tsukita, Ryu Chishu

That Night's Wife (*Sono yo no tsuma*)
Screenplay: Noda Kogo, from a story by "Oscar Shisugoru" (Ozu
    Yasujiro)

Director: Ozu Yasujiro
Director of photography and editing: Shigehara Hideo
Cast: Okada Tokihiko, Yamamoto Togo, Yakumo Emiko, Saito Tatsuo

The Revengeful Spirit of Eros (*Erogami no onryo*)
Screenplay: Noda Kogo, from an idea of Ishihara Seizaburo
Director: Ozu Yasujiro
Director of photography: Shigehara Hideo
Cast: Saito Tatsuo, Date Satoko, Tsukita Ichiro

Lost Luck (*Ashi ni sawatta koun*)
Screenplay: Noda Kogo
Director: Ozu Yasujiro
Director of photography: Shigehara Hideo
Cast: Saito Tatsuo, Yoshikawa Mitsuko, Tsukita Ichiro, Aoki Tomio,
    Sakamoto Takeshi

Young Miss (*Ojosan*)
Screenplay: Komatsu Kitamura
Director: Ozu Yasujiro
Director of photography: Shigehara Hideo
Cast: Kurishima Sumiko, Saito Tatsuo, Okada Tokihiko, Tanaka Kinuyo

1931

The Lady and the Beard (*Shukujo to hige*)
Screenplay: Komatsu Kitamura
Director: Ozu Yasujiro
Director of photography and editing: Shigehara Hideo
Cast: Okada Tokihiko, Kawasaki Hiroko, Iida Choko, Tsukita Ichiro,
    Iizuka Toshiko

Beauty's Sorrows (*Bijin aishu*)
Screenplay: Ikeda Tadao, from a story by Henri de Regnier
Director: Ozu Yasujiro
Director of photography: Shigehara Hideo
Cast: Okada Tokihiko, Saito Tatsuo, Inoue Yukiko

Tokyo Chorus (*Tokyo no gassho*)
Screenplay: Noda Kogo, from a novel by Komatsu Kitamura
Director: Ozu Yasujiro
Director of photography and editing: Shigehara Hideo
Cast: Okada Tokihiko, Sugawara Hideo, Yakumo Emiko, Takamine
    Hideko, Saito Tatsuo

1932

Spring Comes from the Ladies (*Haru wa gofujin kara*)
Screenplay: Ikeda Tadao and Yanai Takao, from an idea by "James Maki"
  (Ozu Yasujiro)
Director: Ozu Yasujiro
Director of photography: Shigehara Hideo
Cast: Shirota Jiro, Saito Tatsuo, Inoue Yukiko, Sakamoto Takeshi

I Was Born, But . . . (*Umarete wa mita keredo*)
Screenplay: Fushimi Akira and Ibushiya Geibei from an idea by
  "James Maki" (Ozu Yasujiro)
Director: Ozu Yasujiro
Director of photography and editing: Shigehara Hideo
Cast: Saito Tatsuo, Sugawara Hideo, Aoki Tomio, Yoshikawa
  Mitsuko
16mm NY

Where Now Are the Dreams of Youth (*Seishun no yume ima
  izuko*)
Screenplay: Noda Kogo
Director: Ozu Yasujiro
Director of photography and editing: Shigehara Hideo
Cast: Ureo Egawa, Tanaka Kinuyo, Saito Tatsuo, Iida Choko

Until the Day We Meet Again (*Mata au hi made*)
Screenplay: Noda Kogo
Director: Ozu Yasujiro
Director of photography: Shigehara Hideo
Cast: Oka Joji, Okada Yoshiko, Kawasaki Hiroko, Date Satoko

1933

A Tokyo Woman (*Tokyo no onna*)
Screenplay: Noda Kogo and Ikeda Tadao, from an idea of "Ernst
  Schwartz" (Ozu Yasujiro)
Director: Ozu Yasujiro
Director of photography: Shigehara Hideo
Editing: Ishikawa Kazuo
Cast: Okada Yoshiko,Tanaka Kinuyo, Egawa Ureo

Dragnet Girl (*Hijosen no onna*)
Screenplay: Ikeda Tadao, from an idea of "James Maki" (Ozu Yasujiro)

Director: Ozu Yasujiro
Director of photography: Shigehara Hideo
Editing: Ishikawa Kazuo
Cast: Tanaka Kinuyo, Oka Joji, Mitsui Hideo

Passing Fancy (*Dekigokoro*)
Screenplay: Ikeda Tadao, from an idea of "James Maki" (Ozu Yasujiro)
Director: Ozu Yasujiro
Director of photography: Sugimoto Shojrio
Editing: Ishikawa Kazuo
Cast: Sakamoto Takeshi, Fushimik Nobuko, Ohinata Den, Aoki Tomio,
    Iida Choko
16mm FI

1934

A Mother Should Be Loved (*Haha o kawazuya*)
Screenplay: Ikeda Tadao
Director: Ozu Yasujiro
Director of photography: Aoki Isamu
Cast: Matsui Junko, Ohinata Den, Yukichi Iwata, Yoshikawa Mitsuko

A Story of Floating Weeds (*Ukigusa monogatari*)
Screenplay: Ikeda Tadao from a film, *The Barker,* by George Fitzmaurice
Director: Ozu Yasujiro
Director of photography and editing: Shigehara Hideo
Cast: Sakamoto Takeshi, Iida Choko, Yakumo Emiko, Mitsui Hideo
16mm NY

1935

An Innocent Maid (*Hakoiri musume*)
Screenplay: Noda Kogo and Ikeda Tadao, from a story by Shikitei Sanseki
    (aka Shikitei Sano)
Director: Ozu Yasujiro
Director of photography: Shigehara Hideo
Cast: Tanaka Kinuyo, Iida Choko, Sakamoto Takeshi

An Inn in Tokyo (*Tokyo no yado*)
Screenplay: Ikeda Tadao and Arata Masao
Director: Ozu Yasujiro
Director of photography and editing: Shigehara Hideo

Music: Ito Senji
Cast: Sakamoto Takeshi, Okada Yoshiko, Iida Choko, Aoki Tomio

1936

College Is a Nice Place (*Daigaku yoi toko*)
Screenplay: Arata Masao, from an idea of "James Maki" (Ozu Yasujiro)
Director: Ozu Yasujiro
Director of photography: Shigehara Hideo
Cast: Konoe Toshiaki, Ryu Chishu, Kobayashi Tokuji, Iida Choko

The Only Son (*Hitori musuko*)
Screenplay: Ikeda Tadao and Arata Masao, from an idea of "James Maki"
   (Ozu Yasujiro)
Director: Ozu Yasujiro
Director of photography: Sugimoto Shojiro
Music: Ito Senji
Cast: Iida Choko, Himori Shinichi, Ryu Chishu, Yoshikawa Mitsuko
16mm FI

1937

What Did the Lady Forget? (*Shukujo wa nani o wasureta ka*)
Screenplay: "James Maki" (Ozu Yasujiro and Fushimi Akira)
Director: Ozu Yasujiro
Director of photography: Shigehara Hideo
Editing: Hara Kenkichi
Music: Ito Senji
Cast: Kurishima Sumiko, Saito Tatsuo, Kuwano Michiko, Sano Shuji,
   Sakamoto Takeshi

1941

The Brothers and Sisters of the Toda Family (*Toda-ke no
   kyodai*)
Screenplay: Ikeda Tadao and Ozu Yasujiro
Director: Ozu Yasujiro
Director of photography: Atsuta Yuharu
Music: Ito Senji
Cast: Takamine Mieko, Saburi Shin, Yoshikawa Mitsuko, Fujino Hideo
16mm FI

1942

There Was a Father (*Chichi ariki*)
Screenplay: Ozu Yasujiro, Ikeda Tadao, and Yanai Takao
Director: Ozu Yasujiro
Director of photography: Atsuta Yuharu
Editing: Hamamura Yoshiyasu
Music: Saiki Kyoichi
Cast: Ryu Chishu, Sano Shuji, Mito Mitsuko, Saburi Shin
vt; 16mm FI

1947

The Record of a Tenement Gentleman (*Nagaya no shinshi roku*)
Screenplay: Ozu Yasujiro and Ikeda Tadao
Director: Ozu Yasujiro
Director of photography: Atsuta Yuharu
Editing: Sugihara Yoshi
Music: Saito Ichiro
Cast: Ryu Chishu, Iida Choko, Sakamoto Takeshi
vt; 16mm NY

1948

A Hen in the Wind (*Kaze no naka no mendori*)
Screenplay: Ozu Yasujiro and Saito Ryosuke
Director: Ozu Yasujiro
Director of photography: Atsuta Yuharu
Editing: Hamamura Yoshiyasu
Music: Ito Senji
Cast: Tanaka Kinuyo, Sano Shuji, Miyake Kuniko, Ryu Chishu

1949

Late Spring (*Banshun*)
Screenplay: Ozu Yasujiro and Noda Kogo, from a story by Hirotsu Kazuo
Director: Ozu Yasujiro
Director of photography: Atsuta Yuharu
Editing: Hamamura Yoshiyasu
Music: Ito Senji
Cast: Hara Setsuko, Ryu Chishu, Sugimura Haruko
vt

1950

The Munekata Sisters (*Munekata shimai, Shin Toho*)
Screenplay: Ozu Yasujiro and Noda Kogo, from a novel by Osaragi Jiro
Director: Ozu Yasujiro
Director of photography: Ohara Joji
Editing: Goto Toshio
Music: Saito Ichiro
Cast: Tanaka Kinuyo, Takamine Hideko, Uehara Ken, Ryu Chishu,
    Yamamura So

1951

Early Summer (*Bakushu*)
Screenplay: Ozu Yasujiro and Noda Kogo
Director: Ozu Yasujiro
Director of photography: Atsuta Yuharu
Editing: Hamamura Yoshiyasu
Music: Ito Senji
Cast: Hara Setsuko, Ryu Chishu, Higashiyama Chieko, Sugimura
    Haruko, Miyake Kuniko
vt; 16mm NY

1952

The Flavor of Green Tea over Rice (*Ochazuke no aji*)
Screenplay: Ozu Yasujiro and Noda Kogo
Director: Ozu Yasujiro
Director of photography: Atsuta Yuharu
Editing: Hamamura Yoshiyasu
Music: Saito Ichiro
Cast: Saburi Shin, Kogure Michiyo, Tsuruta Koji, Miyake Kuniko
16mm NY

1953

Tokyo Story (*Tokyo monogatari*)
Screenplay: Ozu Yasujiro and Noda Kogo
Director: Ozu Yasujiro
Director of photography: Atsuta Yuharu
Editing: Hamamura Yoshiyasu
Music: Saito Takanobu

Cast: Hara Setsuko (Noriko), Ryu Chishu (Hirayama Shukichi),
Higashiyama Chieko (Hirayama Tomi), Yamamura So (Hirayama
Koichi), Sugimura Haruko (Shige)
vt; 16mm NY

1956

Early Spring (*Soshun*)
Screenplay: Ozu Yasujiro and Noda Kogo
Director: Ozu Yasujiro
Director of photography: Atsuta Yuharu
Editing: Hamamura Yoshiyasu
Music: Saito Takanobu
Cast: Ryo Ikebe, Awashima Chikage, Kishi Keiko, Ryu Chishu
16mm NY

1957

Twilight in Tokyo (*Tokyo boshoku*)
Screenplay: Ozu Yasujiro and Noda Kogo
Director: Ozu Yasujiro
Director of photography: Atsuta Yuharu
Editing: Hamamura Yoshiyasu
Music: Saito Takanobu
Cast: Hara Setsuko, Yamada Isuzu, Arima Ineko, Ryu Chishu
16mm FI

1958

Equinox Flower (*Higanbana, Shochiku Kamata*)
Screenplay: Ozu Yasujiro and Noda Kogo, from a novel by Satomi Ton
Director: Ozu Yasujiro
Director of photography: Atsuta Yuharu
Editing: Hamamura Yoshiyasu
Music: Saito Takanobu
Cast: Saburi Shin, Tanaka Kinuyo, Arima Ineko, Sata Keiji
vt; 16mm NY

1959

Good Morning (*Ohayo*)
Screenplay: Ozu Yasujiro and Noda Kogo

Director: Ozu Yasujiro
Director of photography: Atsuta Yuharu
Editing: Hamamura Yoshiyasu
Music: Mayuzumi Toshiro
Cast: Ryu Chishu, Miyake Kuniko, Kuga Yoshiko, Sata Keiji
vt

Floating Weeds (*Ukigusa, Daiei*)
Screenplay: Ozu Yasujiro and Noda Kogo
Director: Ozu Yasujiro
Director of photography: Miyagawa Kazuo
Music: Saito Takanobu
Cast: Nakamura Ganjiro, Kyo Machiko, Sugimura Haruko, Wakao
   Ayako
vt; 16mm FI

1960

Late Autumn (*Akibiyori*)
Screenplay: Ozu Yasujiro and Noda Kogo, from a novel by Satomi Ton
Director: Ozu Yasujiro
Director of photography: Atsuta Yuharu
Editing: Hamamura Yoshiyasu
Music: Saito Takanobu
Cast: Hara Setsuko, Tsukasa Yoko, Ryu Chishu, Sata Keiji, Okada
   Mariko
16mm NY

1961

The End of Summer (*Kohayagawa-ke no aki, Toho*)
Screenplay: Ozu Yasujiro and Noda Kogo
Director: Ozu Yasujiro
Director of photography: Nakai Asakazu
Editing: Iwashita Koichi
Music: Mayuzumi Toshiro
Cast: Nakamura Ganjiro, Hara Setsuko, Tsukasa Yoko, Aratama Michiyo

1962

An Autumn Afternoon (*Samma no aji*)
Screenplay: Ozu Yasujiro and Noda Kogo

Director: Ozu Yasujiro
Director of photography: Atsuta Yuharu
Editing: Hamamura Yoshiyasu
Music: Saito Takanobu
Cast: Iwashita Shima, Ryu Chishu, Sata Keiji, Okada Mariko
vt; 16mm NY

FILMS ABOUT OZU

I Lived, But . . . (Ikite wa mita keredo), dir. Inoue Kazuo (Japan, 1983),
16mm K

ADDITIONAL FILMS CITED

A propos de Nice, dir. Jean Vigo (France, 1930)
Bachelor Party, The, dir. Delbert Mann (United Artists, USA, 1956)
Ballad of Narayama, The (*Narayama bushi-ko*), dir. Kinoshita Keisuke
(Japan, 1958)
Ballad of Narayama, The (*Narayama bushi-ko*), dir. Imamura Shohei
(Japan, 1983)
Banished Orin (aka *Melody in Gray; Hanare goze Orin*), dir. Shinoda
Masahiro (Japan, 1977)
Berlin, Symphony of a City (*Berlin, die Symphonie eine Gröstadt*), dir.
Walter Ruttman (Germany, 1927)
Bicycle Thieves (*Ladri dir. biciclette*), dir. Vittorio de Sica (Italy, 1945)
Catered Affair, The, dir. Richard Brooks (MGM, USA, 1956)
Crowd, The, dir. King Vidor (MGM, USA, 1928)
Double Suicide (*Shinju ten no Amijima*), dir. Shinoda Masahiro (Japan,
1969)
Family Game (*Kazoku geemu*), dir. Morita Yoshimitsu (Japan, 1984)
Gate of Hell (*Jigokumon*), dir. Kinugasa Teinosuke (Japan, 1953)
Idiot, The (*Hakuchi*), dir. Kurosawa Akira (Japan, 1951)
Last Laugh, The (*Der Letzte Mann*), dir. F. W. Murnau (Germany, 1924)
Life of Oharu, The (*Saikaku ichidai onna*), dir. Mizoguchi Kenji (Japan,
1952)
Make Way for Tomorrow, dir. Leo McCarey (Paramount, USA, 1937)
Man with a Movie Camera (*Chelovek s kinoapparatom*), dir. Dziga Vertov
(Soviet Union, 1929)
Manhattan, dir. Woody Allen (United Artists, USA, 1979)
Manila in the Claws of Neon, dir. Lino Brocka (Philippines, 1975)
Marty, dir. Delbert Mann (United Artists, USA, 1955)

Men Who Tread on the Tiger's Tail, The (*Tora no O o fumu otokotachi*), dir. Kurosawa Akira (Japan, 1945)

Mystery Train, dir. Jim Jarmusch (JVC Entertainment, Japan, USA, 1989)

Our Daily Bread, dir. King Vidor (United Artists, USA, 1934)

Paris qui dort, dir. René Clair (France, 1924)

Rashomon, dir. Kurosawa Akira (Japan, 1951)

Solitary Travels of Chikuzan, Tsugaru Shamisen Player, The (*Chikuzan hitori tabi*), dir. Shindo Kaneto (Japan, 1978)

Story of Chikamatsu, A (aka *Crucified Lovers; Chikamatsu monogatari*), dir. Mizoguchi Kenji (Japan, 1954)

Story of the Last Chrysanthemum, The (*Zangiku monogatari*), dir. Mizoguchi Kenji (Japan, 1939)

Straits of Love and Hate, The (*Aienkyo*), dir. Mizoguchi Kenji (Japan, 1937)

Stray Dog (*Nora inu*), dir. Kurosawa Akira (Japan, 1949)

Sunrise, dir. F. W. Murnau (Fox, USA, 1927)

Travel Chronicles of Yaji and Kita (*Yaji-Kita dochuki*), dir. Chiba Yasuki (Japan, 1958)

True Heart Susie, dir. D. W. Griffith (Studio, USA, 1919)

Ugetsu (*Ugetsu monogatari*), dir. Mizoguchi Kenji (Japan, 1953)

White Threads of the Cascades (*Taki no shiraito*), dir. Mizoguchi Kenji (Japan, 1933)

Reviews of *Tokyo Story*

TWO INCHES OFF THE GROUND

LINDSAY ANDERSON

Reprinted by courtesy of the estate of Lindsay Anderson.

After 1930, the Japanese cinema turned to sound, and confined itself to the filming of traditional plays or imitations of Hollywood. Work of social significance disappeared. . . .
(George Sadoul, *History of the Cinema*)

Well we (and no doubt M. Sadoul as well) know better now. And not merely as a result of the few Japanese films – all post-war – that have been commercially distributed in the West; not merely through enthusiastic reports from festivals, and informative articles in *Sight and Sound* – but now, at last, from the films themselves. This wonderful season at the National Film Theatre has been, of course, only a start; but at least six thousand or so people in London have now had the opportunity to see for themselves that Kurosawa has a range that extends far beyond the exotic and the violent; to experience the work of great directors like Mizoguchi, Ozu and Gosho; to become acquainted, in short, with a whole tradition of film-making of which Western historians of the cinema have, up to now, been perfectly ignorant – and which must in future basically affect any of those generalisations we are all so fond of making about "The Cinema."

145

For instance: "Movies have got to *move.*" One of the things these Japanese directors have made clear to us is that our interpretation of this precept has been a great deal too facile. They almost persuade us, in fact, that movies are best when they don't move at all. More seriously, they oblige us to reconsider and re-define what we mean by movement. (And here, it is interesting to note, their calm example seems to confirm the most interesting and daring ventures of Western avant-garde work in recent years.) For in the West, "cinematic movement" has usually been related to our experience of the theatre, in effect if not in style. "Cinema is not literature." And in the name of this principle almost all the world's great novels have found themselves simplified, sharpened, streamlined and betrayed by translation to the screen. Of course, we too have had our anti-theatrical prophets: most consciously, I suppose, Bresson. But it is in the work of these Japanese directors that we see at its richest and most developed a conception of cinema where the relationship of the artist to his public is far nearer that of the novelist to his reader than that of the *metteur-en-scène* to his audience. This is not quite the same thing as being "literary." Imagine, when you have seen *Ugetsu Monogatari* or *Chikamatsu Monogatari,* an *Anna Karenina* filmed by Mizoguchi. It is not merely that he is a finer artist than the Western directors who have taken the subject; it is that the method, the *wholeness* of his vision can create a whole world, in which detail and atmosphere are as significant (contribute as much to the "movement") as the characters-in-action, the plot.

Probably of all these directors, Kurosawa is the most Western in his attitude – one might almost say the most modern (without implying that the others are old-fashioned in any pejorative sense). And presumably this is why he has been the first to become anything like a celebrity in Europe. But his *Ikiru,* which we should call *Living* (the proper translation) and not *Doomed* (which is a silly, distributor's title), comes as a fascinating revelation after the more brilliantly surfaced *Rashomon* and *Seven Samurai*. It is a modern story, and we start simply, directly, without dramatisation. The screen is filled with an X-ray photograph of the principal character's chest. He has got cancer, a voice tells us. And we see him, an elderly, desiccated little man, a civil servant, sitting behind his desk, methodically applying his seal to a pile of papers – which obviously arouse in him not the slightest attention or interest. Deliberately and in detail this man's situation and story are explored. He learns that he can expect only six months more to live, and with this discovery comes the realisation of the complete meaninglessness of his life. His work is without purpose; he has sacrificed everything for his son (he is a widower), to whom he is nothing but a nuisance and a potential source of a legacy. Nowhere in his life can he find anything of the slightest significance: a night spent despairingly in pursuit of joy, in bars and brothels, only leaves him sick and exhausted. It is the ebullient, spontaneous office-girl, who has left her job in disgust to go and work in a toy-factory, who gives him his answer. "Why are you happy?" the wretched man asks: and in her simplicity she tells him. Her toys are a pleasure to make, because she can think of the pleasure they give. And for the last tortured months of his existence, the man finds purpose and fulfilment by accepting the responsibility of his position and forcing through the indolent and corrupt bureaucratic machine a scheme for the construction of a children's playground on a waste area in the city.

Whether there is a deficiency in the central performance of this story, or whether the awakening and change of direction by the principal character is too arbitrary, I am not sure: but I am conscious of (to me) a certain lack of conviction in the total effect. But what is more to the point, and richly suggestive, is the whole method of the film; the bare force of its style, the awareness and relevance of a whole social background, the edge and sharpness of its characterisation. Perhaps most striking is Kurosawa's conception for the last half of the picture. Instead of being recounted as a straight narrative, the process of the park's construction (naturally, once it is completed everyone gets the credit for it except the true originator) is pieced together in flashbacks from the dead man's funeral, where his family, colleagues and superiors sit ceremoniously together, discussing him in varying terms of hypocrisy, misunderstanding or (in one case only) sympathy. Here Kurosawa's clear-sighted, analytical view of human nature is at its most telling, and the deliberate, piecemeal tempo at which the reconstruction is taken is completely at variance with conventional ideas of "How to Construct a Screenplay." In comparison with *Living*, in fact, *Umberto D.* seems hardly experimental at all. It is almost incredible that films of this seriousness and weight can be produced within the framework of a commercial industry. Too often, it is clear, the cinema is credited with limitations which are in fact not the limitations of the medium at all, but simply the limitations of the cultures within which Western film-makers have had to work.

In comparison with Kurosawa, both Mizoguchi and Ozu seem traditionalist in feeling and style. Both were famous in the silent cinema of Japan – Ozu, in fact, fought shy of sound as heroically as Chaplin; his last silent film was made in 1934. But this traditionalism does not make their films inaccessible, though perhaps it does demand slightly greater readjustment from a Western audience. Both are austere directors – in Mizoguchi's case this is less obvious in *Ugetsu*, where the tale itself is so full of marvels, than in *Chikamatsu*, where the restraint of the style is only rarely broken by the exciting use of Kabuki music, or a sudden, eloquent movement of the camera. In *Tokyo Story*, the camera moves only three times from the beginning to the end of the picture, and then with the most gentle discretion; and in this film particularly, the whole concept of "pace" (with which, significantly, Western film-makers are so apt to be obsessed) is not so much different from ours as irrelevant. This is an extremely important point, and one which must be understood if the best of the Japanese cinema is to be appreciated as it deserves. And so, for the rest of this piece, it is of *Tokyo Story* that I shall write – with no insult intended, of course, to Mizoguchi. But surely both *Ugetsu* and *Chikamatsu* will be shown again, and written about in full.

Tokyo Story is not a good title: the American *Their First Trip to Tokyo* is better, since it at least manages to suggest the theme and emphasis of the film. The story is not about Tokyo, but about two old people, living a good way from the capital, who come to see their two grown-up children who are now working in the city, as well as the young widow of another of their sons. They spend a few days there, but soon realise that their children have grown away from them, and that they are more tiresome than welcome. Only the daughter-in-law, a sweet, unhappy woman living by herself, receives them with real affection and generosity. On the journey home, the old lady becomes ill, and they stop off for a day with another of their sons, a clerk on the railway. Home again, with their youngest, still unmarried daughter, the illness becomes serious; the children are sent for; the old woman dies. The children return to Tokyo, and the father remains with his daughter. . . .

It is a film of relationships, a film about time, and how it affects human beings (particularly parents and children), and how we must reconcile ourselves to its working. Apart from the great fact of death, the incidents are all slight, and there is no chiaroscuro either in characterisation or mood. The tempo is all the way calm, leisurely, inevitable. There is only one element in the style which might seem at first to jar: the sequences do not fade into each other or dissolve. Every transition is effected by a cut, to some view of the new setting, a rooftop, a wall, a harbour vista, which then cuts again directly to the scene where the characters are going on with their living. But this is not jarring: on the contrary it is a way of conveying the essential unity of existence, of matter and spirit, which is intrinsic to the film's philosophy.

> . . . The Taoist mentality makes, or forces nothing, but "grows" everything. When human reason is seen to be an expression of the same spontaneous balance as the natural universe, man's action upon his environment is not felt as a conflict, an action from outside. Thus the difference between forcing and growing cannot be expressed in terms of specific directions as to what should or should not be done, for the difference lies primarily in the quality and feeling of the action. The difficulty of describing these things for Western ears is that people in a hurry cannot feel.

This quotation from Alan Watts' recent introductory study, *The Way of Zen*, seems to me to describe exactly the feeling of *Tokyo Story* – and the difficulty of explaining it to those who find (like some film society secretaries) that it is "too long" and that "nothing happens." For what we have here is a work that expresses in every image, and in the precise *growth* (as opposed to *force*) of its movement, a whole attitude to living, an attitude that comprehends, in the sense of both understanding and embracing, the painful necessities as well as the joys of existence. From our point of view this philosophy can be called, at least partly, humanistic; but this is by no means its essence. And it is here, I think, that even a reviewer as appreciative as John Gillett (in *Film*) is in danger of missing the point. For with all its understanding and compassion, *Tokyo Story* is not a simple humanistic protest against the transience of life and the bitterness of experience. Specifically, in the "marvellous shot" (which it is) "of the tottering figure returning to the house and the mourners" it is *not* the "inner grief" of the old man that is being symbolised, but rather his wisdom and acceptance. For what has he just said to the girl who has just hurried out to be with him? He has remarked placidly: "It was a beautiful sunrise. I think we're going to have another hot day." Surely here many people in a Japanese audience would remember Basho's poem:

> How admirable
>   He who thinks not "life is fleeting"
>   When he sees the lightning.

Even more than its humane virtues (I know one ought not to attempt the differentiation), it is the directness and clarity with which *Tokyo Story* reflects a whole philosophy of living that makes it so memorable an experience. For this reason I have chosen to illustrate it, not with a dramatic or "beautiful" shot, but with a sequence which may convey something of its method and its quality. The funeral is over, and the children have gone back to Tokyo. The old man is saying goodbye to his daughter-in-law: he has given her a watch as a memento of his wife. "It's funny," he says, "but though we have children of our own, you are the one who has been kindest. Thank you." She cries; and we hear the voices of children singing; the song goes to the tune of "Massa's in the Cold, Cold Ground." (The overlap of sound is like something out of *Diary for Timothy*, and the poetic implications are the same.) The school-house: a corridor, at the end of which passes a line of children. Then the classroom, where the youngest daughter is teaching. From the window she sees the train go past, carrying the daughter-in-law back to Tokyo. Then just railway lines, empty.

However hard its artists have tried, the cinema has never seemed satisfactory as an intellectual medium. Perhaps Zen Buddhism, anti-conceptual, and as unhesitating in its acceptance of the world as it is basically anti-materialist, has a particular relevance to film making.

And my title? Alan Watts writes: "When Professor D. T. Suzuki was once asked how it feels to have attained *satori*, the Zen experience of 'awakening,' he answered, 'just like ordinary, everyday experience, except about two inches off the ground.' " Progressive filmmakers of the West have always tried to make men feel that, by keeping their feet firmly on the earth, they can still be ten feet tall. This is not, I think, just another way of saying the same thing. Or can we have it both ways? Here is an important question these films invite us to ponder. Its implications spread considerably wider than the screen: but that, after all, is what the cinema is for.

TOKYO STORY

STANLEY KAUFFMANN

The British film journal *Sight and Sound* conducted an international poll last fall asking critics to list their ten favorite films of all time. On my list – and on four others – was *Tokyo Story* by Yasujiro Ozu, made in 1953. I first saw it last spring in the Japanese retrospective at the New York Museum of Modern Art. Now *Tokyo Story* is having its first theatrical release in the U.S. I've seen it again, and I'm happy that it was on my list.

Ozu made fifty-four films, of which only a handful have been released in this country. I have seen only three besides this one. He was born in 1903, died in 1963, and is one of the two best Japanese directors I know, the other being Akira Kurosawa (*Rashomon, Ikiru,* etc.). In his own country Ozu is called the most Japanese of directors, and a Westerner can see at least a little of why this is so. But that is a defining, not a limiting, comment. (Who is more Swedish than Bergman?) There is treasure for everyone in *Tokyo Story* – and shame that we have all had to wait so long for it.

The films of Ozu's last period, the ones I know, tend toward a *largo* tempo, and are crystallized in loving but austere simplicity. Kurosawa, a fine artist, is an immediately exciting director; Ozu, a fine artist, is not. Kurosawa is essentially a dramatist, Ozu a lyric poet whose lyrics swell quietly into the epic. Of his four late films, all of which have beauty, *Tokyo Story* is the most successful.

The reader may find it hard to believe that a wonderful work could be made from this story. An elderly couple who live in the south of

Japan, with their unmarried schoolteacher daughter, go to visit their married children and their grandchildren in Tokyo. During their visit they also see their widowed daughter-in-law, whose husband was killed in the war eight years before. Then the old couple return home, and the old lady sickens, badly. The children gather at her deathbed. After her death, they go home, and the old man is alone.

This material makes a film of two hours and twenty minutes. It also makes a film that encompasses so much of the viewer's life that you are convinced you have been in the presence of someone who knew you very well. Students of mine were asked recently to write papers on what they know about Chaplin. One of them began: "I don't know how much I know about Chaplin, but he certainly knows a lot about me." That seems to me one excellent definition of superior art, and it applies to Ozu. As for his societal remoteness, the most obvious and fundamentally the truest point about Ozu is that by being "most Japanese," he has been universal.

The beauty begins with the script, written by Ozu and Kogo Noda, who collaborated with him through most of his career. Chishu Ryu, who plays the old man and who acted in very many Ozu films, said (*Sight and Sound,* Spring 1964):

> Mr. Ozu looked happiest when he was engaged in writing a scenario with Mr. Kogo Noda, at the latter's cottage. . . . By the time he had finished writing a script . . . he had already made up every image in every shot, so that he never changed the scenario after we went on the set. The words were so polished up that he would not allow us even a single mistake.

Other good directors often work otherwise. With Ozu the result is not mechanical execution of a blueprint but the fulfillment of a design. He knows that when a passing neighbor wishes the old couple bon voyage at the beginning, the same neighbor will speak to the lonely old man at the end. He knows that, when he shows us a baseball uniform hanging on a clothesline outside a son's window, it will later tie in thematically with the daughter's class of children singing Japanese words to a Stephen Foster tune.

The subjects dealt with in this film are the subjects of soap opera – with one crucial difference. As the film starts, as we "locate" its components and its movement – the trip to Tokyo – we expect that there will be dramatic developments. *There are none,* except for the death of the old woman very near the end. A lesser film maker would have thought: "Now what complications must I devise to keep things interesting?" Ozu, with Noda, thinks only: "What are these lives like? Really like?" And by holding to truth, much more than to naturalism, he gives us a process of mutual discovery, the characters' and ours.

In Tokyo the old couple learn that their doctor son is not quite the success, nor quite the man, they imagined; and that their married daughter has been coarsened into a penny-biting, suspicious shopkeeper. The breath of love they did not expect is from the daughter-in-law, who is still bound to her dead husband's memory, although both she and his parents know that he wasn't the most admirable of men. In responsive concern, it is they, the dead husband's parents, who urge her to remarry.

Three instrumentalities give this film its exquisite cinematic texture. First, the acting. Ryu, the bent, faintly ludicrous, somewhat egocentric, truly dignified old man. (With a partiality for drink – Ozu understands contradictions.) Chieko Higashiyama, his wife, quite homely, who – like Eleanor Roosevelt – becomes *facially* beautiful as her spirit is manifested. Setsuko Hara, the daughter-in-law, tall, ungainly, humane (one feels) partly out of fear to be selfish, out of fear of desire, but nevertheless humane.

Then there is Ozu's punctuation. As a composer uses rests or holds a chord, he puts in a shot of an empty street after a busy scene, or a railroad track, or a small ship passing, or an empty corridor in a house. This gives us time to let what has just happened sink in even further and helps to place it. The world, imperturbable, surrounds the perturbations of its people.

Third, inevitably, Ozu's eye. His famous characteristic is the "Ozu shot," the camera placed at the eye level of a person seated on a *tatami,* the Japanese floor mat. Much of the film is seen from this "national" viewpoint, even when characters are standing. That's perhaps as much a matter of psychology as of vision. Ozu's vision gives us such compositions as the stout old woman and her little grandson silhouetted on a hilltop; the old couple seated on a curved sea wall at a resort outside Tokyo, seen from behind, tiny but together against the illimitable sea; or the camera moving slowly past a pavilion in a Tokyo park until, around the corner, we see, again from behind, the old couple seated, eating their lunch – a moment of inexplicable, deep poignancy. In these scenes and many others, Ozu seems to be saying: "These are atoms. In any one atom is the universe. My task is not to dishonor the universe by honoring these atoms."

Symmetry is important to him but never becomes tiresome. Two pairs of sandals outside a hotel bedroom door, precisely placed, show that two people, en route through their lives together, are spending this particular night behind that door. On a larger scale, he balances sequences. At the beginning, the parents travel to the children; at the end, the children travel to the parents. In Tokyo the old woman and the daughter-in-law have a scene alone together, a very moving one in which the old woman spends the night in the younger woman's small apartment while the old man is out drinking with some pals. At the end it is the old man who has a scene alone with the daughter-in-law, after his wife's death. He tells her that his wife said her night in the apartment was her happiest time in Tokyo, and he gives the girl the old woman's watch as a keepsake.

Which raises the subject of scale. Everything in the film is calibrated with such refinement that feelings are always restrained but never lost, so that when, near the end, the girl takes the watch and cries quietly, the effect is of a tremendous emotional climax.

If I had to choose one word as the theme of *Tokyo Story,* it would be "passage." Time passing, life passing, with the ache and (if we admit it) the relief that this implies. Out of the loins of these two people whom we see sleeping quietly side by side came the children who are now turned away from them, and we know it will happen to the children with their children; and the old people know it and, without saying so, are content to have had what they have had and to have been part of the process.

If I had to choose one word to describe Ozu himself, it would be "purity." Like the Dreyer of *Joan of Arc,* the Bresson of *Diary of a Country Priest,* Ozu gives us the sense that questions of talent and ambition have been settled or forgotten, that he is now self-centered in what can be called a selfless way. In *Tokyo Story* he is placing on the screen the very least that will fulfill the truth of what he has seen. There is no brave consciousness of integrity. He is simply consecrated to serving life simply, and proudly.

TOKYO STORY

ROGER GREENSPUN

I am not sure how to introduce yet again a director who died nine years ago, whose name should be familiar to all film lovers, but who remains virtually unknown – except to say that *Tokyo Story,* another great movie by Yasujiro Ozu, opened yesterday at the New Yorker Theater. Made in 1952, it is the earliest of the three (out of more than 50) Ozu features that have so far had local premieres.

Even on the basis of a limited exposure to his work, the story seems archetypal Ozu. An old couple living in the southern Japanese port city of Onomichi take their first trip to Tokyo, to visit their married children. The children – a neighborhood doctor and a beautician – are tolerant, but preoccupied and a little put out by the old folks' visit, and only a non-relation, the widowed daughter-in-law of their son lost in the war, makes them feel welcome.

After several days and a few small adventures, the parents return home. But on the train the mother takes sick, the children are summoned and shortly afterward she dies, surrounded by her family, "peacefully, without suffering, and full of years," in the words of her somewhat disagreeable married daughter. The daughter-in-law stays the longest after the funeral, but eventually even she must leave, and the father settles quietly into the loneliness that is to be his life.

It is important to remark the characteristic look of the Ozu movies – the product of an almost immobile camera usually shooting from a low position, and the absolute rejection of such sleights of cinema as the fade or the dissolve – and to note that this look is in itself an example of the seemly patience the films mean to invoke. *Tokyo Story* really deals with three generations passing through life, but mostly with the generation that is passing out of it, and it understands that a calm reticence may be the true heroism of ordinary old age.

"Isn't life disappointing," observes the family's younger daughter, an unmarried schoolteacher who lives at home. "Yes, it is," answers the daughter-in-law, and the two of them smile with a cheerful, slightly embarrassed sense of misery. An anthology of Ozu's scenes of shared understanding between young women would constitute one of the glories of world cinema. But in context this scene, very near the end of *Tokyo Story,* essentially completes a view of normal life that is luminous in its freedom from the sentimentality or the satire that so often obscure an artist's vision of normal living.

Ozu will sometimes return to a room or a passageway, now empty, where, a few moments earlier, people had been seen. It is not nostalgia, so much as an acknowledgment that places are sanctified by people and that even when they have gone away, a bit of their presence lingers on.

Those people, at least in *Tokyo Story,* are marvelous and they are played by actors so wholly of their parts that it is all but impossible to think of them in other roles in other movies – though they do in fact make up part of an Ozu stock company.

Just for the record I should like to give credit to Setsuko Hara as the gracious daughter-in-law; Chiyeko Higashiyama as the mother; and Chishu Ryu, surely one of the most beautiful actors in Japanese film, as the father who lives so gently beyond his time.

A MASTER FROM JAPAN

CHARLES MICHENER

From *Newsweek,* March 27, 1972; © 1972, Newsweek, Inc.; all rights reserved; reprinted by permission.

An elderly couple travel to Tokyo to visit their married son and daughter. Too busy with their own lives to offer more than token hospitality, the children shunt them off to a spa. But the spa is too noisy, and the parents return to Tokyo and then home, where the mother falls ill and dies, leaving the father to face his last years in loneliness.

Like a Japanese paper flower that is dropped into water and then swells to fill the entire container with its beauty, this most minimal of plots becomes a shattering, universal drama of family tensions in *Tokyo Story,* a neglected, nineteen-year-old masterpiece by Yasujiro

Ozu, the Japanese director who died in 1963. Hailed by international critics as one of the best films of all time, the work is only now receiving its first U.S. commercial showing, under the auspices of New Yorker Films, which plans national distribution to introduce Americans to one of the great, original film artists.

Fallen

"Less is more" was the essence of Ozu's artistry. With *Tokyo Story* he described the coming apart of the family system in postwar Japan. Yet his approach was that of a miniaturist to whom disclosure of character was sovereign to social criticism. A spoiled grandson swivels angrily around in his father's office chair – and sums up the rebelliousness of his generation. The shop-owning daughter berates her husband for buying expensive pastries – and reveals the dominance of materialism in her generation. The old father turns back to help his fallen wife, who then picks herself up unassisted – and Ozu says all about the interdependence and dignity of their traditional relationship.

But there is a higher achievement as well. "Ozu illuminated the mundane to bring out the transcendental," says film scholar Donald Richie, who has just written a full-length study, *Ozu: The Work and Life of Yasujiro Ozu,* published by University of California Press. When the old father responds to his wife's death by quietly remarking, "I'm afraid we'll have another hot day," the illumination is overwhelming.

Ozu's style was as restrained as his content. In *Tokyo Story,* there are no optical effects, no fades or dissolves, but only a succession of scenes shot by a stationary camera from the same position – about 3 feet above the floor, the vantage point of a haiku master kneeling on his tatami mat. Quick cuts for dramatic effect were equally taboo. Scenes are played out as though they have an organic life of their own, and the film proceeds with the formal, stately pace of a Noh drama.

Yet the effect is not cold or boring, but intensely involving. Ozu's patience with his characters ("He was afraid of *using* them," says Richie) induces one to be similarly respectful; his steady, clear-eyed vision heightens the viewer's own attention to detail. The mother's slow lowering of herself on her tatami mat at bedtime tells everything about her disappointment with her children. "I want to make people feel without resort to drama," Ozu once said, and his success should bring today's nervous, angle-happy cameramen to their knees.

Identity

Because of his austerity and his unremitting devotion to contemporary "home dramas," Ozu was considered "too Japanese" for widespread export – though his spare approach is shared by such Western giants as Robert Bresson and Antonioni, who once called Ozu the most avant-garde of directors. Yet, throughout his long career – he made 54 films between 1927 and 1962 – he was Japan's most honored director, outstripping even Mizoguchi and Kurosawa. A lifelong bachelor, he was a legendary perfectionist who worked out every detail of the script before shooting, and personally designed the décor of each scene. The shooting was just as painstaking. Scenes were reshot endlessly, often because a performer's inadvertent movement had marred the over-all composition, and Ozu's control over his actors was absolute. Chishu Ryu, the great character actor who plays the old father in *Tokyo Story,* once said: "I cannot think of my own identity without thinking of him."

Though Ozu's method was totally unspontaneous, his characters live as few characters in movies do, as though Ozu's camera had simply found them going through their lives. It is only one of the many paradoxes about the great Japanese humanist whose tombstone epitaph sums up his life – and art: the single character *mu,* which literally means "nothingness," but which in Zen philosophy implies "everything."

———

SOMETIMES THE TWAIN

PENELOPE GILLIATT

The name of Ozu, the great Japanese director, is probably memorable to Westerners because it has only three letters to recall instead of nine or ten, or because it sounds like the Greek drink spelled backward. His masterpieces are less well known. He made fifty-three films in his lifetime (1903–63). Most of us have seen few. Chance to repair. His wonderful *Tokyo Story* (1953) is now at the New Yorker. The queues curl round the block.

Yasujiro Ozu is often called a miniaturist, maybe because he didn't move the camera and because he dealt with domestic detail, but he was no more a miniaturist than Chekhov was. The observer who keeps quiet is the one who picks up the big storms, perhaps. *Tokyo Story* is a calm-surfaced tale of an aging provincial couple visiting their mildly ingrate children in Tokyo. By shunning plot, as usual, Ozu gives dense energy to story. The picture is *Lear* with the sting of rage drawn but without any feeling or extremity lost. The couple sense that the course of their past is being put to the test, and they find it wanting. Ozu always catches his characters at moments when they are driven to their limits. Life is difficult for most people, he says, and most people make a fair job of it. Their opportunities for heroism are restricted, and I think he would see heroism as lying in moments of not being as irresolute as at other times. A lot of fiction now, especially in movies, shows us cocksure mannikins whose tone comes from the teller; Ozu presents people who are chronicled as more or less noble or intelligent or able, and who move freely in and out of the frame of the director's temperament. The concrete expression of that freedom, making his photography look sometimes a little like Renoir's, is there in the way he will show us a shot of an empty room, take his time observing it before some child scampers through in the background or a neighbor looks briefly in at a window, and then leave the shot as empty of people as before. The habit says something powerful about place as being sanctified by people and endowed with their natures long after they have skipped off to play, or died.

Ozu is obsessed with film's possibility of reporting the poetic truth of the actual. He is reality's artisan, and its connoisseur. The dialogue of his films seems as solid as what one sees. Kogo Noda was the writer he worked with first, and on many, many of his best pictures, including *Tokyo Story*. Even in subtitling, the lines of the scripts that he wrote with Kogo Noda have the weight of beautiful strange coins that one wants to hold in the hand. It strikes me as very like Ozu's tone in his film dialogue that this passionate apprentice of minimal gestures and brief, idiosyncratic remarks should have said flatly once that he was devoted to "big things, like whales." His favorite scriptwriter obviously shared his feeling. Their work together has a minuteness that is often Olympian. The stories are concerned mostly with the middle to upper of the hundred strata in Japanese society, and they show us worlds in small facts of life that have a dash of oddity about them. *Tokyo Story,* like Ozu's *Late Spring* and *Good Morning* and *Late Autumn,* speaks with moral brilliance about parents and children, about a modernized traditional society falling apart, about young people with a bewilderingly lower ceiling of aspiration than the ones nearer to the finish.

The couple, grandfather and grandmother, are coming to Tokyo from quite a long way away. There is agreeable fuss about a thermos to travel with, and an air cushion. The grandfather is played by Chishu Ryu, who is practically a member of the Ozu stock company: a gentle old man with a mustache, whose beneficent constant smile eventually comes to express to us as many variations of contentment, joy, absorption, and grief as there are fractions of tone in Japanese music. A friend pokes her head in at the window to say, "Your children have turned out well." But the children, when it comes to seeing them, are subtly less than the parents, with smaller aristocratism and grace. One is a beautician, one a doctor. There is a lack of serenity in the children that seems to reflect a fall in social class, or even to explain it. In Tokyo, the preparation for the old ones' visit has been gnawed now and again with tetchiness. There has been much talk among the grownups of being busy, and the grandchildren have caught the mood; a schoolboy grandson, for instance, has had a tiff about his desk's being moved for the couple's stay, and he has taken shelter in a comically dignified pretense of being hard-pressed by homework.

There is a widowed daughter-in-law of great sweetness who works in an office. "How clever, earning your own living," says the grandmother simply. The greetings on the grandparents' arrival remind you only of Chekhov, as so much in Ozu does; there is the same mixture of verbal abruptness and delicacy, the same small eddies of contradiction, the same funny rudeness that is possible only between the oldest intimates. The grandmother is told by her daughter that she has grown taller since the day when she broke a chair under her long ago – and fatter, too. "Oh, no. That chair was already broken." The old lady hadn't realized Tokyo was so near, she says. Yet it is in fact a very long way from home in her head. Later, the couple talk together on their own. They came far after reaching the railway station; they must be in a suburb, they decide, wondering how well their children have really done. The weather is hot and still. People use paper fans to stir breezes, sitting with their other hand on their knees. Grandchildren itch in the atmosphere of adult inertia and sit swinging their legs in an agony of stalemated energy. The grandmother takes a very small grandchild in a sun hat for a walk: there is a marvelous long shot of them on a hill, over some of Ozu's rarely used music. "What are you going to be when you grow up? A doctor, like your father?" The child doesn't answer, is just glad to be out. The more cautious middle generation discusses the economics of whether it is better to have crackers or cake today. There are touching flurries of grown-up planning to go to a public bath and buy some ice cream on the way back. The widowed daughter-in-law is eventually asked to take the old people off the grown children's hands by acting as guide to them on a tour of the city. The trip, by bus, goes splendidly. The old man wears a straw hat and looks beguiled.

Sent soon afterward to a health resort, in another bid by the bored careerists to be rid of them, the grandparents fret against the honeymoon features of the place and find the amusements noisy. One night, gently maddened by jolly music, they both sit up from their beds on the floor bolt upright. (The old man is perpetually convinced that his wife sleeps like a log; she tends always to insist that she had a bad night.) Let's go home. Where's home? The welcome back in Tokyo is fractious. You're back so soon. Was it crowded? A bit crowded. The old man decides to visit some cronies and is privately bent on getting drunk, which he does with distinction and the utmost in the irritating to his children, who swat away the elegant reemergence of his long-ago comfort in boozing as though it were a mosquito. The old man is seeing friends whom he hasn't met for seventeen or eighteen years. Very slowly – with the slowness of the assault of the warm *sake* – they slide into talk of children. One of them admits that he is in the habit of lying about his son's success and calling him a department head when he's only a group leader; other men's sons have a doctorate. Ah, well. Young men in general today have no backbone. Spare the rod and spoil the child. Some sons would kill their parents without a thought. The lenient kings slither into outraged stupor and stumble back to their

Gonerils and Regans, who receive them rattily. The beautician daughter, a housewifely woman, hates the sight of her father drunk as if he were a dusty floor; the censorious doctor son seems inclined to call a hangover a warning of trouble to come. It is a theme of the film that the young, with half their lives to go, turn out to spend them more stingily than the old, one of whom is shortly to die.

The charity and distress reflected in Ozu's view of people is a characteristic of absolute steadiness, like the way he uses his camera, which barely moves from its low-set position through any of his films. There is never a pan shot and only very rarely a dolly shot. In *Tokyo Story*, the grown-up children's moments of crabbed behavior are only an aspect of them. Things pass, people change, says the film. A loss is irreparable; all the same, one grows used to it. Both things are true. The old man, left alone at the end of the picture after his wife's death, is both unconsoled and consoling. Yes and no are less polar in Japan than in the West. He gives the widowed daughter-in-law his dead wife's watch. It's old-fashioned, he believes. Romantic love was never Ozu's interest; intimates' love, always. The impulses in his films are tender and complex. (Moments in *Tokyo Story* recall the scene in his *The End of Summer* in which a garrulous cousin complains what a nuisance her relative's funeral is, and then suddenly bursts into tears.) Ozu has a genius for saying serious things lightly, and he seems preoccupied by the idea of spiritual survivors: in *Tokyo Story* there are two, and the old one is paradoxically intent on expanding the life of the young one.

The close physical limits Ozu chose to work in were obviously a goad and a joy to him. In the thirties, while he was making some of his most brilliant comedies, he was the last great director to begin to use sound (not until 1935–36). Even then, it seems, he came to it because he liked the notion of a stationary microphone as a way of further confining his actors' moves. As early as 1932, he had given up dissolves and fades. The editing of his films is a flawless example of phrasing in art. His later pictures are technically the most strictly controlled I have ever seen. The physical facts of them celebrate restraint and simplicity as much as the content does. In his stories, his inclination was more and more to show us the world in a family; this is not the Western philosophy of the individualist but the philosophy of man in society, and society is the family. Everything in his work is precise and palpable. Ozu is interested in the spiritual force of things as they are, of man in accord with his surroundings. The outside world is not something to be conquered, as it is in the West; it seems almost an annex of the self. An incident in an Ozu film is not a report of an accomplished fact but something in progress, occurring in a flux of time that flows serenely and makes an eternal present even of the remote past. The firmness, pity, and humor of his films' smiling regard for his characters are together one of the manifest miracles of cinema.

TOKYO MONOGATARI (TOKYO STORY)

TONY RAYNS

Reprinted by permission of *Sight and Sound.*

The elderly Shukichi Hirayama and his wife Tomi live in retirement in Onomichi, a port on Japan's Inland Sea, with their younger daughter Kyoko. They undertake a trip to Tokyo to visit their son Koichi and daughter Shige, both married and with families of their own; they also plan a brief stop-over in Oskaka to see their younger son Keizo. On arrival in Tokyo they stay with Koichi, a paediatrician, and are soon conscious of disrupting the household; Koichi's wife Fumiko is a model of formal politesse, but the elder son Minoru resents giving up his study to provide an extra bedroom and the younger son Isamu takes the opportunity to be even more mischievous than usual. The only person who welcomes them with selfless sincerity, despite her straitened circumstances, is their daughter-in-law Noriko, wife of their son Shoji, missing presumed dead in the war. The major family event planned to mark their visit, a Sunday excursion, has to be cancelled at the last minute when Koichi is called away to a patient.

Shukichi and Tomi move on to stay with Shige, who runs a hair salon in the front room of her home. Her husband Kurazao has no idea how to entertain the visitors beyond buying them desserts and inviting them to the public bath, and Shige, reluctant to spend money on them, asks Noriko to take a day off work to show them around Tokyo. The sightseeing trip is a success, and that evening Noriko invites the couple to her modest home. Shige and Koichi decide to share the cost of sending their parents to the hot-spring resort Atami for a few days, to get them off their backs. The old couple enjoy Atami at first but after a sleepless night listening to rowdy young people in the hotel decide to return to Tokyo immediately. As they prepare to leave, Tomi suffers a dizzy spell.

Their early return inconveniences Shige, who has invited guests for dinner, and so Tomi goes to spend the evening with Noriko while Shukichi looks up his old friend Osamu Hattori. Late that night the police escort Shukichi, Hattori and their friend Sanpei Numata to Shige's home; all three are incapably drunk after an evening spent reminiscing and discussing the disappointments of parenthood. Next day the entire family gathers at Tokyo Station to see off the old couple on their return home.

But they spend the next few days at Keizo's home in Osaka, after Tomi is taken ill on the train. And they have hardly got home before Kyoko is sending telegrams to her brothers and sister to say that Tomi is gravely ill. Koichi and Shige reluctantly but dutifully rush to Onomichi with their mourning clothes, closely followed by Noriko. All are present when Tomi dies; Keizo arrives just in time for the funeral. At the wake, Shige disgusts Kyoko by demanding various of her mother's effects. Koichi and Shige return to Tokyo without delay, and Keizo remembers a baseball game in Osaka that he wants to catch. Noriko is left to console Kyoko, who is furious at the attitudes and behaviour of her siblings. In saying goodbye to Noriko, Shukichi urges her to forget her late husband and remarry while she has the chance; he gives her Tomi's prized pocket watch as a keepsake. Kyoko, a primary school teacher, is at work when Noriko takes the train back to Tokyo. Shikuchi is left to face the future alone.

Ozu described *Tokyo Monogatari* as his "most melodramatic" movie, an observation taken by most Western commentators, dazzled by the director's minimalist style and resolutely quotidian material, as ironic. But irony was never Ozu's preferred tone, and his comment surely reflected the film's uncharacteristic explicitness: this is an almost didactic film about the disintegration of Japanese family values, full of characters and incidents designed to spell out social and psychological points with diagrammatic clarity. In calling the film "melodramatic," Ozu may also have had in the back of his mind the story's origin in co-writer Kogo Noda's memories of the

1936 Leo McCarey film *Make Way For Tomorrow*, which similarly contrasts the emotional stoicism of an elderly couple financially ruined in the Depression with the brash impatience of their urbanised children but does so with a directness entirely normal in Hollywood movies.

Although it is not a precise match with any other Ozu film in theme, tone or structure, *Tokyo Monogatari* obviously shares characteristics and concerns with many of them. Its interests in parent–offspring relations, in urban–rural contrasts, and in the evanescence of happiness are all entirely consonant with earlier films, from *Hitori Musuko* (*The Only Son*, 1936) through conservative wartime films like *Toda-ke No Kyodai* (*Brothers and Sisters of the Toda Family*, 1941) and *Chichi Ariki* (*There Was a Father*, 1942) to other films of the postwar "reconstruction" like *Banshun* (*Late Spring*, 1949) and *Banushu* [*sic*] (*Early Summer*, 1951). It also uses most of Ozu's well-known visual tropes, from the use of low camera-positions for domestic interiors to patterns of cutting based on visual analogies rather than conventional eyeline-matches. What's different here, is, again, the overall explicitness of the film's aim. The fact that this is a film in which the main characters frequently and directly discuss the issues that confront them (for example, parents' disappointment in their children's levels of assessment, or a young woman's disgust at her elder sister's uncaring meanness) militates against both the psychological nuancing and the structural playfulness that Ozu elsewhere used freely.

In part, the film's overt seriousness springs from its persistent undercurrent of social commentary. This is absolutely a film of its moment: it faithfully records everything from Tokyo's post-war rebuilding boom to the raucous and hedonistic behaviour of young people in a hot-spring hotel, the latter an early sign of the "Sun Tribe" delinquency that was to become Japan's hottest social topic only three years later. (Since Ozu and Noda habitually retreated to hot-spring resorts themselves to work on their scripts, it's amusing to speculate that they themselves had experienced the same kind of sleepless night suffered by the Hirayama couple.) Equally topical was the core theme of the chasm between traditionalist, rural parents and their city-based sons and daughters; the breakdown in age-old family support structures in the years of American occupation and "democratisation" was a widely discussed topic in the early

1950s. And the financial plights of Koichi and Shige, one struggling to run a suburban medical practice, the other managing a tawdry hair salon, both in conspicuously unfashionable areas of the city, are observed with the same fastidious eye for social and economic demographics.

The characters are also somewhat less nuanced than in many other Ozu films, even when played by the directors' favorites from the Shochiku "stock company" of contract actors. Haruko Sugimura's account of Shige, for example, is a nakedly explicit picture of the death of sentiment: the woman is a cypher for selfishness, opportunism and greed. Ozu allows himself one set-piece of comedy (in an otherwise generally sombre movie) at her expense: the scene in which she is embarrassed to have her drunken father and two equally comatose strangers dumped on her late at night by the police. The chief exceptions to this tendency towards caricature are Shukichi, the emotionally repressed patriarch played by Chishu Ryu, and Noriko, the more than dutiful daughter-in-law played by Setsuko Hara, Japanese cinema's "perennial virgin." Shukichi's feelings for his wife are expressed only silently, in wordless scenes after her death, while his only avenue for open discussion of his frustrations as a parent is while drinking with long-unseen buddies in a bar. Noriko, shown to be both a hyper-efficient "office lady" and a model of selfless consideration, is given dialogue scenes (most notably with Kyoko and Shukichi, in quick succession at the film's climax) to admit her inner doubts and insecurities, especially in relation to her fidelity or otherwise to her late husband. Both actors achieve the deepening of their characters with practised ease and supreme conviction.

Aside from Taizo Saito's lush but sparingly used Hollywood-style score, the film's soundtrack is dominated by three elements: chirping crickets, boats chugging and sounding their sirens, and train noises. The crickets evoke the rural ambience of Onomichi, while the other two sound elements evoke travel and the space between places – and by extension, people. But Ozu is far too subtle and humane an artist to reduce his sound design to a matter of schematic symbols. In a film concerned with constant journeying, it's significant that the only shot of anyone in the act of travelling is the image of Noriko on the train back to Tokyo in the end. In the shot, she pulls out Tomi's heirloom, the pocket watch, and examines it with deep emotion. The shot mysteriously clinches the association between the idea (or sound) of travel and the motif of evanescence. This may be the least "melodramatic" moment in the film. It is also probably the most truly Ozu-esque.

Select Bibliography

Anderson, Joseph, and Donald Richie. *The Japanese Film: Art and Industry*. rev. ed. Princeton, NJ: Princeton University Press, 1982.

Bock, Audie. *Japanese Film Directors*. Tokyo: Kodansha, 1978.

Bordwell, David. *Ozu and the Poetics of Cinema*. Princeton, NJ: Princeton University Press, 1988.

Buehrer, Beverley Bare. *Japanese Films: A Bibliography and Commentary, 1921–1989*. Jefferson, NC: McFarland, 1990.

Burch, Noel. *To the Distant Observer: Form and Meaning in the Japanese Cinema*. Berkeley: University of California Press, 1979.

Geist, Kathe. "Narrative Strategies in Ozu's Late Films." In *Reframing Japanese Cinema: Authorship, Genre, History*. Ed. Arthur Nolletti, Jr., and David Desser. Bloomington: Indiana University Press, 1992.

"Playing with Space: Ozu and Two-Dimensional Design in Japan." In *Cinematic Landscapes: Observations on the Visual Arts and Cinema of China and Japan*. Ed. Linda C. Ehrlich and David Desser. Austin: University of Texas Press, 1994.

McDonald, Keiko I. *Cinema East: A Critical Study of Major Japanese Films*. East Brunswick, NJ: Associated University Presses, 1983.

Richie, Donald. *Japanese Cinema: Film Style and National Character*. Garden City, NY: Anchor, 1971.

Ozu. Berkeley: University of California Press, 1974.

Sato, Tadao. *Currents in Japanese Cinema*. Trans. Gregory Barrett. Tokyo: Kodansha, 1982.

Schrader, Paul. *Transcendental Style in Film: Ozu, Bresson, Dreyer*. Berkeley: University of California Press, 1972.

Index